What Others A
Living in Grace

"Beca Lewis' new book will more than 'shift' you—it will send a bloody tsunami your way! Read and open your heart. Read and prepare for abundance!"
—Joline Godfrey, CEO, Independent Means, Inc.

"A Refreshing and powerful new look at the results of shifting perceptions to your true spiritual nature."
—Alan Cohen, author of 24 books including The Dragon Doesn't Live Here Anymore

"Beca's book reminds us to adjust the view of life and naturally, shift will happen - in all the very best ways. A wonderful and practical guide to living life in amazing grace!"
—Susan Gilbert, New Media Strategy Consultant, Best Selling Author and Entrepreneur

"Shift to Spiritual Perception and you will change your life! Perception does rule, and in the everyday and spiritual use of this truth as so succinctly and clearly revealed in this book, you will fulfill your promise and achieve your destiny. Wow!"
—James Wanless, PhD, author of Voyager Tarot and Intuition@Work

"I could say the book is terrific and it is. But better than terrific, the book is important. It is important in that everyone should read it. The message of the book presented with conviction is that thoughts are things and we need to watch what we think for the good of ourselves and mankind. Ms. Lewis gets down to what is probably real, what is core, and that therefore makes an important book...better than merely a terrific book."
—Warren Gruenig, CEO

Living In Grace: The Shift to Spiritual Perception
by Beca Lewis

Published by: Perception Publishing
Cover Design: Elizabeth Mackey

Copyright © 2002 Beca Lewis
All rights reserved.
ISBN-13: 978-0-9719529-0-4

Library of Congress Cataloging-in-Publication Data
Lewis,Beca.
Living in grace:the shift to spiritual perception: a
guide to personal practical spirituality/by Beca Lewis
    Includes bibliographical references
    ISBN -10:0-9719529-0-6
    1.Spirituality. 1. Title
    BV4501.2.J.492002 248.4
    QB102-701495
    Library of Congress Control Number: 2002104649

LIVING IN GRACE: THE SHIFT TO SPIRITUAL PERCEPTION

A Guide to Personal Practical Spirituality

Beca Lewis

Dedication

To my children, Charles, Christin, and Laurie, and grand-children, Madison, Montana, Cassidy, Logan, and Maxton and Del's children, Del, Jessie, John, Mesa, and Michael, who teach me so much about true love.

To my sister, Jamie, and my sister-friends, who have supported and believed in The Shift®, and in me, as we have grown and developed through the years.

To my husband, Del, who by sharing his special knowledge and awareness, fills in the gaps of The Shift® and my life. Del reveals balance, harmony and the knowledge of true substance to all who know him. This book was completed and sustained through Del's wisdom.

To Dorothy Hardy, my mentor and best friend, who believed, long before I did, that I could and would help to make spirituality practical for others, but first demanded that I make it practical in my own life.

Thank you Dorothy, wherever you may be—this is for you and for all the years you believed in me, and for your demonstration of Living in Grace.

Contents

THE SEVEN STEPS TO SHIFT

Step One—Be Willing

Step Two—Become Aware

Step Three—Understand Signs and Symbols

Step Four—Learn Perception Rules

Step Five—Shift To Spiritual Perception

Step Six—Walk As One

Step Seven—Celebrate With Gratitude

PREFACE

This book is about perception and how to shift our perception to Living in Grace. This Shift of Perception will demonstrate the truth that we are all living as and in Grace now. There has never been a single moment that we have not or will not be Living in Grace. However, in this place I will call the "Earth state of mind" there appear to be paths that we must walk to remember this fact. On these paths, we search for meaning, power, and reasons for our existence. Most people in the Earth state of mind walk the "material path."

On this path the Earth, the universe, and everything we are and do is material. In the material world perception, physical power reigns.

Some of us have "upgraded" to the "mental path" of believing it is a mental world, and everything is within and of our own thinking. We use mind-power to accomplish our goals and live a better life. In this point of view, the mind-body connection comes into play. We begin to say, "I can do it! All I have to do is visualize enough, and get my mind and thinking straight." Mind-power employs methods such as visualization and hypnotism to accomplish its goals. This mental path will sometimes diverge into another path, the path of mysticism.

The world today is fascinated by this mental or mystical power and is calling it the "Spiritual revolution". Talk of God is accepted, and is now found in all walks of life.

It is an improved point of view over the physical standpoint, but it is not the path where this book will take you.

There is one more path—and it is the path of One Mind, that path of non-power, the true Spiritual path. This is The Shift to being completely conscious that all that we are, know, and see, is in truth Spiritual. This is Living in Grace.

It is hard to write a book about spirituality and make it practical at the same time. I have to use physical words and mental exercises to make a point. Sometimes I talk about "getting things" or "improving your life."

However, getting things and improving one's life is a result of the consciousness that this is a Spiritual universe, not my reason for writing this book. Getting things and improving life is not the point. An improved life is the fruit of the awareness of, and the living out of, the Truth that there is only One—of everything—and that One is Spirit. It is the choice to Shift to Spiritual Perception.

The Shift to Spiritual Perception explains the power of perception. It is our point of view, our perception that determines our world and the life we lead. This book presents *The 7 Steps To Shift* and an eight step-by-step system based on the word GRACIOUS, which makes the necessary process of perception-shifting easy to remember and simple to use.

The book is an attempt to bridge the belief system of living in a physical world to the actuality that everything is actually spiritual. It is the best I know as of this moment. I know it to be true that it is a Spiritual Universe and that Heaven is here and now, because it is part of my experience.

How to remain in that consciousness, and how to communicate this understanding, is the path that I appear to be traveling.

There is no place on any path to stop and say, "I know it now, there is no more to learn." Even as I write this book I am yielding, or dying, to the old "point of view" and improving my consciousness of the Spiritual One.

Follow the guidance in this book only as it appears as Truth to you. Use this book to guide you, but it is not Truth itself. As you use the tools in this book to change your point of view and your state of mind, you will find this out for yourself, and we will reunite together in the awareness of Grace.

SECTION ONE

Spiritual Perception

Chapter One: Perception Produces Reality

If the doors of perception were cleansed, everything would appear to man as it is, infinite.
—William Blake

Have you ever wondered what your life would be like if everything you ever thought came true? You could think of true love and within moments the doorbell would ring and your personal true love would be standing on the doorstep, ready and able to begin to live a life full of love just with you. Perhaps you would think of having more money than you could ever spend, and once again the doorbell would ring and on the doorstep would be a box full of money.

The truth is we do have our thoughts come true. So why don't we have all we've ever wanted? Why are so many of our lives filled with "quiet desperation"? Why don't we live with constant unlimited abundance?

Perception produces reality and what is perceived to be reality magnifies.

The answer is powerful and simple. We receive in our lives exactly what we believe to be true and what we believe we deserve. In order to live the life we were meant to live we must change our point of view and focus on the Truth of our Being.

All shifts are a decision to change a point of view. The Spiritual Shift is the continuous moment-by-moment personal, conscious, choosing of Spiritual Reality over the cramped, limited belief in many personal realities.

It is the decision not to believe or act out of duality or separation.

As we are willing to choose to become conscious of, and remain in the awareness of Grace, our ego-based small-i thoughts disappear and are replaced by Divine Mind's Thoughts. As a result, we recognize the material universe, as it really is —Spiritual Reality—and who we really are, the reflection of the One.

Isn't it a perfect time to follow your irresistible movement toward the Divine and yield to the State of Grace?

What will happen as you read this book? There is no guarantee that your life will be better. There is no guarantee that money will flow in the door and everybody will love you. This is not "no-work" solution to the problems in your life. Choosing spiritual consciousness makes great demands upon us.

What will happen is that you will find a focus that will make world success both meaningless and a natural event. Your life will change. Not because you want it to, not because you are trying to prove something, fix something, or get better at something.

It will change because you have chosen to take the time to do the only important thing in life. You have chosen to take the time to change your focus and build your own personal inner conviction of the existence of the State of Grace.

Possibilities are an outgrowth of a Shift of Perception to what is beautiful, good, and true. Life is abundant when we celebrate it from the Source and not from the outcome.

You must be the change you wish to see in the world.
—Mahatma Gandhi

The world is now too dangerous for anything less than Utopia
—R. Buckminster Fuller

On this planet there are something like five billion human beings, so there are five billion perceptions of reality. Everyone can be looking at the same object, but seeing it very differently.... One's perspectives, one's view of things determines...how one experiences change, life, and the purpose of life.
—Dalai Lama, Gathering Sparks

Small r reality or big R Reality?

Belief systems are now being defined in the language of physics and other sciences. But science is not saying anything new. It is simply restating those views that were understood in different words and symbols thousands of years ago.
—Bob Tober, Space Time and Beyond

Your assumptions are your windows on the world. Scrub them off every once in a while, or the light won't come in.
—Alan Alda

I remember when I first became really interested in what I call big R Reality. When I was about seven years old, I was in the neighbors' yard playing ball with their dog. The ball was a large white softball and the grass had just been mowed. It was early evening and I knew that I had to be home before the streetlights went on, but I pushed the time limit by throwing the ball up one more time. Neither the dog nor I saw it come down. I was worried, because being late was not an option. The dog and I ran all over the yard looking for the ball. If I had been a dog, I would have been barking as frantically as he was.

Finally, I stopped in the middle of the yard, put my hands on my hips stomped my foot and said, "OK God, I know you know where this ball is, so I want to see it right now!" I looked down and the ball was at my foot.

I had no time to be surprised. Instead, I snatched up the ball and ran home. Later, when I had a chance to think about it I asked myself…"Hummm, did that ball come out of a Twilight Zone episode?" You know, where each scene of our life is constructed "back stage." Perhaps someone had forgotten to put the ball back into that scene, and added it when I asked to see it. Or…was that ball always there and I just couldn't see it because of my state of mind?" My seven-year-old brain did not phrase it quite that way, but that was the essence of the question.

I have come to see that the ball was already there. My state of mind kept me from seeing it just as our state of mind and a belief system sees through the hole of our point of view rather than seeing the whole of what is already ours, already present.

My point of view…shifted!

Without being fully aware of it, I had started
a lifelong search to understand how the ball "just"
appeared. What I discovered for myself, as many have
before me, is that everything has already been created.
We already have everything we could ever need or want.
What we receive from this infinite supply is what we
perceive to be reality. The most limiting thought of all
is that we receive only what we believe we deserve to
receive.

How did it get this way? In this state of mind, we call
"living on Earth," we have accepted a substitute version
of Reality. This can be called the small r reality. We use
this personal paradigm as the guide, or pattern, for our
standard of living. It is how we define ourselves.

There is only one Truth. We are unlimited Spiritual
beings. However, in this Earth state of mind, instead of
living in Truth, we live a dream story about limits and
evolution. We call this world material. We say things
about this world, like "this is how it is." Or: "If God had
wanted us to (fill in your favorite saying)…, He would
have given us…"

We are living in an age where we can hook up to a
computer-generated program and live an event as if it
were real. Our thoughts, emotions and sensations react
to what the computer is giving to us. This is called virtual
reality.

Now imagine for a moment that the life we live is
just us hooked up to a program that we believe through
and through.

Like virtual reality, it feels, tastes, smells and acts upon us as if it were real. But it is not. As we shift our viewpoint, we can shift our virtual reality to Reality. Just as disconnecting from the computer program releases us to "reality," disconnecting from the program of our training and culture releases us to Reality.

Isn't it exhilarating and freeing to know that the only thing that needs to change is our point of view, our belief? Let's begin together to leave behind the old and take up the Truth, using the Seven Steps to Shift as our guides.

Chapter Two: Principles of The Shift®

The First Step To Shift—Be Willing.

He who would may reach the utmost height, but he must be eager to learn.
—Buddha

Are you willing to be aware of the abundance, in all its forms, that already is present? Are you willing to let go of the beliefs that hold you and bind you to a sense of lack? Are you willing to become what you are meant to be? Are you willing to be worthy?

The single most important key to The Shift to Spiritual Perception is the first step of Being Willing. There is no way around this first step. Being Willing cannot be forced on anyone or faked.

Being Willing involves every moment and every thought. It includes being willing to let go, willing to do what is asked, willing to be open, willing to set boundaries, willing to have no desires, willing to have everything, willing to follow inspiration, willing to wake up, willing to stop hurting, willing to be happy, willing to not be liked, willing to be loved, willing to let Truth be the one and only guide—all these are examples of willing.

We must be willing for anything to happen. If we are not willing, nothing will ever be accomplished. We will either not start, or we will sabotage the effort. To be willing we must yield and let go of our own ego and our thoughts of how it ought to be. If we are going to move to an unlimited Reality, we must desire to see the Truth, no matter what the cost to our cherished beliefs.

This willingness is not about applying human will. Any time we force an issue by using the human ego and will, we are heading down a path that will eventually bring trouble. Although it may accomplish the immediate purpose, we have lost the larger goal of moving towards unlimited abundance and Truth.

It is our human perception of ourselves that has limited us in the first place. Human will carries us only so far before letting us down. Human will blinds us to what is true. Our desire is to be willing, not willful.

The process of Shifting is the preparing of the human mind to consent. Our task is to teach our mind with logic and love to let go. We are not attempting to make our small minds better. We are in the process of asking our human mind our—self-perception, our personality, the voice inside who says "this is me" — to step aside and yield to the larger unlimited Mind.

We do not change our minds; we release them. We learn to yield to a full and loving picture. This picture benefits all it touches. Our own small picture will usually benefit only us.

Being willing also applies to how we deal with others. We cannot force other people into anything unless they are willing.

Think of all the heartache we would save ourselves and those we love by simply noticing whether they are willing to do whatever we are asking them to do, and if they're not, by letting them work it out in their own way. All we can do for those we love is to provide a place where they feel it is safe to be willing.

Cross the cow gate.

Our willingness lies in our ability to step past our fears. In the movie "Camilla," Jessica Tandy plays the role of a woman who has a chance to step forward into a life that she has dreamed of for years. Since she had originally come from the country, she describes a cow gate as an obstacle that keeps the cows from wandering out of the pasture.

It is not really a gate and there is no fence, just boards laid into the road. The cows, not liking the feel of the boards, will not cross this gate even though there is nothing really keeping them in. By the end of the film, she does step through her personal cow gate into her new life.

What keeps us in our unfenced pasture and not moving on to our dreams are things we think we do not like to "step over," or things we do not want to do. It could be as simple as not wanting to make a phone call. It is not the large things or actions that keep us from our dreams; it is the small things that we are not willing to do that impede our progress.

Once we are willing to move to unlimited reality, either these little things melt away or we gain the courage to cross over the willingness threshold into an unlimited life that has always been awaiting our return.

There is neither an end nor a beginning to Being Willing. It is the constant conscious yielding to Truth, which is Heaven here and now.

Even if you are on the right track, you will get run over if you just sit there.
—Will Rogers

The Second Step To Shift—Become Aware.

Awareness is an art. In its purest form it is the ever-expanding constant consciousness of the State of Grace. In small r reality, awareness first brings to light the belief in two opposite points of view called "good" and "bad." These opposites appear in every area of life. If one group of people says something is good, another group believes just the opposite. In small r reality our minds create both good and evil states. We plan, scheme and try to make things happen. In Reality, what we perceive as our minds are avenues for awareness, through which divine ideas flow.

Our lack of awareness keeps us at one end of a point of view in a distorted, conditioned mind, which is out of balance and at odds with the other end. Awareness of Reality brings the understanding that one is no better than the other, and that the belief in opposites or separation is a product of human conditioning. To release our small minds it is often necessary to become aware of our current physical, emotional, and mental states to uncover hidden thoughts and habits, which keep us from experiencing the State of Grace.

Change your life question or statement.

Each of us has a "life question or statement" that we continually say to and about ourselves. That question or statement colors everything else that we see and think. Although it is called a "life question or statement", it usually keeps us in a state of "death" or the inability to see and live Life as we were meant to live it. It is a belief about how the world works.

This belief is an outgrowth of the life we think we are supposed to live, which was created by our conditioned worldview. To experience a totally abundance-filled life, our current life question must be uncovered and replaced with one that serves and expands our perception instead of limiting our life.

The question or statement we say or ask is usually not evident to us, but it is certainly evident to our friends and family. To find the belief that is determining your point of view, ask someone who loves you what it is you keep on saying.

Here are some examples of common life questions that many people continually ask. The wording may be different but the meaning is the same.

• Why is life so unfair?
• Why is life so hard for me?
• Why do other people have all the luck?
• Why doesn't anybody love me?
• Why don't I know what to do?

No matter what the question is, it is framing the outcome of our life, because what we believe to be reality magnifies. Every time the question is asked, the reality it is manufacturing becomes more entrenched.

A few years ago, I decided consciously to choose my own life question(s). The object was to stop unconsciously listening to an old limited life question and switch to one that would help me to consciously experience the presence of Grace.

I made up a few questions to ask myself that would remind me to move away from the limited point of view of myself, to who I really am and the life I was meant to live.

The changes I found myself making without a forceful effort were astonishing. I still ask myself the following questions consciously a few times a day—especially when I am making any kind of decision.

- Am I running?
- Am I hiding?
- Am I lying?
- Am I waiting?

There is no right or wrong to the answers. What they provide is awareness. Once aware, we can choose to rise above this limited point of view, and Become Aware of the place of the One—or the still place—the State of Grace.

The Third Step To Shift—Understand Signs and Symbols.

Matter is matter only to the material state of consciousness, but once we rise to a mental state of consciousness, matter is not matter, but mind.
—Joel S. Goldsmith, The Thunder of Silence

The outside, visible world is the projection of the internal and non-visible world of our point of view. The signs and symbols of the universe are not the Truth but messages that can be interpreted to discover either the essence of the Truth they are revealing or the lie they are telling.

Signs and symbols make up every part of life—from traffic to nature. Being Aware of the difference between signs and symbols of what is True and the reversal of what is True is critical to understand. Signs and symbols are not anchors but guideposts on our path. If we believe them to be real and Truth rather than signs and symbols, we will be locked into the accumulation of things rather than be free to be the full expressions of boundless Life.

In the Chapter Unkink The Hose, we will further discuss how to observe and use signs and symbols to become more aware of belief systems that govern our perception of reality.

Light—as symbol.

Whenever I look into a mirror now, I think of the light. I know that I am seeing only a small fragment of my own totality. The figure staring back at me is the barest representation of what is there and what I may actually be.
—Joe McMoneagle, Mind Trek

Quantum physicist Arthur Zajonc says, "Understanding the true nature of light requires looking not only with the eyes, but with the soul." He and a friend designed an exhibit as part of a science project he called "Eureka." It consisted of a box with a projector whose light shown directly into the box without touching any part of the box.

Obviously within the box was pure light. However, when they looked through a view port into the box there was only blackness. When they inserted a wand, it revealed the light by reflecting it back. Without an object on which light can fall, there is only darkness.

We take light for granted. We think it is part of our world. But it is not. It is part of an invisible world, like the wind. Both are only visible in their interaction with an object.

God, like the light and wind, is invisible. God is always invisible. Without us—God's reflection—God would not be apparent. Everything we see is a result of God, the abundance of God, the supply of God, but not God Itself.

Quantum physics—as symbol.

What quantum mechanics says is that nothing is real and that we cannot say anything about what things are doing when we are not looking at them. Nothing is real unless it is observed... and we have to accept that the very act of observing a thing changed it.

—John Gribbon, In Search of Schrodinger's Cat: Quantum Physics and Reality

The chair on which you are sitting is constructed out of fundamental laws, rather than out of such material objects as atomic particles—an almost theological concept.

—Allen D. Allen, Does Matter Exist? The Foundations of Physics

Physics describes the behavior and idea of energy, which is still a material element.

However, the essence of physics can take us further into an understanding that this is in Reality a Spiritual world.

Those of us who are not physicists can take the easy way out by considering physics in a way that it will be helpful to Shift out of our point of view. Quantum physics informs us that everything is a wave until it is observed. Then it turns into a particle. What does that mean? First of all the word "observed" in this context means "think about."

Quantum physics is saying that there is nothing "real" until we think about it; then it becomes solid (real) to us. Therefore, every moment is new if we choose to live it in Reality.

This idea explodes ruts! It means that the moment we change what we're thinking, or what we believe to be true, our world changes accordingly. Why don't we see this? We will discuss the answers to that question later—but for now just a hint. Could it be we have a habit of holding on to our point of view so that we can hold on to who we think we are? Quantum physics reminds us that we cannot separate the observed from the observer. The dream and the dreamer are one.

The computer—as symbol.

The discovery of how our DNA is put together rocked the world. The implications of this breakthrough are interesting and bring to mind the thought of "how we are like a computer," or how the computer is a symbol of Truth.

Now that we know the order of the DNA sequence, scientists are able to understand which part of the DNA strand to "fix" or "change" to produce the results they might want—like perfect health, or intelligence.

Looking at it simplistically, it means they will fix the bugs in our computer programming, and perhaps continually upgrade our software. By plugging into their system, we will hopefully become better in all ways.

Instead of reacting either way to this idea, look at it as a symbol of what is true spiritually.

What if we understood that what appears to be a material DNA is really a spiritual idea? What if we understood that the main computer is really Divine Intelligence—or One Mind—and that our personal computer system is part of the One Computer System called God? This One Computer is always expressing perfection. As we become aware of this perfection our world, appears "upgraded."

Our "free will" has given us the choice to believe that we are separate from Mind, God, or the One Computer. But believing it does not make it so. The moment we remember— wake up to, experience, think through, and know—that we are not separate, our DNA bugs disappear; because it was our sense of being separate that produced the illusion of "bugs" in the first place. As we wake up to the Truth of our connection we experience an upgraded, newer and better understanding of who we really are.

The Internet—as symbol.

Connecting to the Internet is a wonderful symbol of connecting to the Kingdom of Heaven. How?

First—look at how we get on-line to the Internet. We use a connection service. Which one do we use? There are many choices. Does it matter which one we use? Not really. We determine the parameters that we are comfortable with to get on-line. But we will eventually all get there if that is where we are choosing to go.

Should I judge how you make your connection? Should it be important to me, which one you use?

Should I punish you if you use the wrong one, or assume that you will be punished because you use one that is different from mine? No. Neither should we be judging the way or the method that others choose to reach the Kingdom of Heaven. It is their choice. Each one of us walks a different path, but if the intention is clear, we will all eventually connect. Of course, for me, I want the fastest, clearest, simplest, and most service-oriented way possible.

Once we get to the Internet, how is it like the Kingdom of Heaven? Check this out—we are all there and it is each person's unique contribution that makes it actually exist. We get more and more out of the Internet as more of us contribute and participate. It is our unique expression of an idea that brings it to life—whether it is the Internet or the Kingdom of Heaven.

Like the Internet, the Kingdom of Heaven is impartial. It does not know whether we are male, female, beautiful, or ugly. It exists because we exist. It is our point of view that creates what we see of either one.

What else is the same? Some of us say we can't "do" the Internet. Some of us say we can't "find" the Kingdom of Heaven. Again, it is a matter of simply looking and seeing that both are here now.

To see and use both, we need to clear out and let go of habits and thoughts that keep us in the rut of our current thinking of how it is and then we can choose the Kingdom of Heaven.

We may argue that the Internet has serious problems. There are some really terrible sites (sights) and many people who find pleasure in trying to destroy our joy in it. And so—what is different here? Who is doing this? People and their choices are producing this result.

The Internet as an idea is not doing any of this. It can't. A negative, and sometimes evil, point of view attempts to use this impartial idea to express what is not good, but the idea of the Internet itself remains impartial.

What can we do about the negative side? Start by choosing not to participate or give power to the negative symbol of the Internet. Stop being interested (either because we are curious or disgusted) at those things that appear to be bad or evil. Set boundaries. Protect yourself. Don't believe the point of view that says things are not good now. Dial up. Get in. Participate. Share. Express yourself. The result? We all experience an improved version of a symbol of the Oneness and expression of the Kingdom of Heaven.

The Fourth Step To Shift—Learn Perception Rules.

There is one "law" in the physical universe that can never be overturned or negated. The law that "Perception produces reality and what is perceived to be reality magnifies." And its corollary:

"An error in the premise must appear in the conclusion."
—Mary Baker Eddy, *Science And Health With Key To The Scriptures.*

Our point of view produces the visible. We verify what we believe through our senses and then agree that what we have verified is reality. With this agreement our personal reality reproduces itself again and again. Every reproduction creates a stronger belief.

Belief produces emotion. Emotion strengthens our belief and the cycle continues.

Nothing we experience is how it "really" is. Everything we experience is the out-picturing of our highest understanding of Truth. We are seeing our "point of view" and calling it reality.

The reality rut.

Something that keeps us from stepping over our personal cow gate are the ruts we live in. What is a rut? A rut is something that happens over and over and over again in much the same way. The more we do and live in the rut, the deeper it gets. We live in ruts because we are so busy taking care of our daily lives we think we don't have the time or energy even to examine the ruts—let alone step out of them.

We get into ruts because we have forgotten that what we believe to be reality magnifies. We look at the reality we have created by our own thinking, and think again that it is real. Our belief strengthens. After all, we can see, feel, taste, and touch it, and get emotional about it. With each confirmation we receive from the outside world saying that lack and limitation are true, our rut gets deeper.

A newly sighted person, blind from birth, does not immediately see the people and things around him. He first sees light. From there he "learns" to see by listening and touching what is already familiar. In time, he sees the form. We know that after being given their sight, some people decide it is easier to stay blind, and revert to sightlessness.

Isn't this decision just like most of us sometimes? We perceive a new truth and begin to move towards it. But, it involves work, and what before seemed so difficult and limiting now becomes the easier path to take. We retreat to the familiar of what we already know.

However, we deserve more. Rut living is not what we were designed to do. It is not our purpose. Our purpose is to express our personal talents and gifts as an unlimited Spiritual being, not to be bound to the sense of lack inherent in rut living. We can Shift our thoughts into high gear, an expanded view, and accelerate into abundance.

To get out of any rut we have to Shift our beliefs about what is real. This is a Shift in thinking. Whatever we shift our thinking to becomes our reality. When you Shift your point of view, the world Shifts with you. Why is this true? Because the world we call "real" exists only in our own perception.

Welcome to spaceship Earth.

Paradigm: Pattern: an outstandingly clear or typical example. A philosophical and theoretical framework of a discipline within which theories, laws, generalizations, and the experiments performed in support of them are formulated.

Point of view = paradigm = rut:

Ruts (paradigms) are dug inch by inch, even before we are born. Those eagerly—or not—awaiting our arrival are preparing both the mental and physical ground for our life. They begin by projecting whom we will look like. They attach hereditary beliefs to us. They envision our future. They already either like or don't like the impact we are having and will have on their own lives.

Once we are born, it is almost as if we have crash-landed in alien territory. We are totally new to the life system in which we find ourselves. No matter what our family or culture, the lifestyle is already set up and we must learn to adjust and fit in. We began to understand what works and what doesn't. We adapt in order to survive and hopefully to thrive.

We hear what people say about us and about how the world works, and we believe it. We decide to agree with what we are learning about being here at this time, in this state of consciousness we call Earth, because we want to fit in. In time we forget what we knew before we "landed": that we are Spiritual—not material—beings. We start believing the current system of reality, whatever it may be. We have accepted the worldview. The master hypnotist—our culture—has us hypnotized.

We must change the way we see the world. We are in a crisis of perception. What we need is a new vision of the world.
—Fritjof Capra, The Turning Point

The eye refuses to see what the mind does not know.
—Deepak Chopra

How ruts work.

Ruts, a.k.a. paradigms, filter information. They provide evidence to us that tell us this is how life is, so don't bother asking for more. Or they prove to us that we were always right, so therefore we have nothing more to learn. When we say, "This is who I am," we are stating our paradigm.

A paradigm operates in much the same way as a computer file. The computer will feed back anything that has been put into it. It cannot receive, let alone understand, any information that does not fit exactly within parameters. When we go to the memory banks and pull up the file called "father," for example, we will see on the screen everything we have told the computer about father, nothing more.

The most important function of a paradigm is to act as a filter. Every bit of information that comes to us is filtered through our paradigm. Only the information that fits into what is defined by the paradigm (such as home, country, spouse, parent) comes through. We never know about most information available to us because the paradigm says "no."

Most of the time, our paradigm does not allow us the chance to make a decision about what we think we want to know. However, if the paradigm called "me" is broad enough to let the information reach a decision level, we will still "consciously" filter according to our idea of who and what we are and who we are capable of being.

We will say "no" to anything that does not fit our belief system. If there is any other reality available to us, we are effectively kept from knowing it.

At this point, we are the paradigm.

Sometimes we demand more. We attempt to change our mind, or change the paradigm. To change we agree to enlarge or Shift our point of view. How do we do that?

Going back to the example of the computer file "father:" If we want a larger picture of "father" we must supply the computer with more information. We cannot go to the computer to get that information, as it can only tell us what we already know. Once we gather additional information from other sources and add it to the database, the file (paradigm) is expanded.

For example, most of us have experienced the expanding or shifting of a paradigm when we decide to buy a car. Have you ever noticed that as soon as you begin to think about a certain kind of car you see them everywhere? What happened? Did the company begin to manufacture more of these cars and somehow they magically arrived on the streets just for us to see? Obviously they were already there. We just expanded our paradigm—our point of view—enough to see them. This was a Shift in thought.

The lies our senses tell.

You will see it when you believe it.
—Wayne Dyer

How does a person learn to sing if he's never heard a song, doesn't know about words, melody and pitch; worse, if he doesn't know he has a voice?
—Robert Monroe

Awareness is the source of the seeing.
—Deepak Chopra

What gives us the information regarding our perception of what we call reality? Our senses. What they report back to us we take as literal truth. If we can see, hear, taste, feel, or smell it—it must be true.

But let's step back. Since everything starts in thought and then becomes what we believe to be reality, then it follows that all our senses are doing is reporting back what we have thought to be real, not what is real. What we call reality is a phenomenon resulting from the way our thought focuses to create an incomplete awareness.

This idea often shows up symbolically in the world. For example, while reading this page we think that we are reading the black letters. In reality, we are seeing or reading the white light. Black is the absence of light. To read we focus on the negative or the absence of light as if it were real.

This is what we do in life. We focus on what appears as the absence of a good quality such as "love" and see "hate" and believe that it is real. When we learn to focus on what is real, what is unreal vanishes, because it never existed in the first place.

Fight or flight is another example of learned behavior that must be unlearned if we are to become conscious of Reality. In our human past, it was necessary to react to a negative event by either fighting or fleeing. We had to remember the negative to survive. The cave dweller absolutely needed to link the sound of a snapped twig with the possibility of a bear approaching because he had to either fight the bear or flee from it. We have carried that focus with us throughout human history, even when we don't need it. We continue to focus primarily on the negative. It is that focus that maintains its existence—nothing else.

Our Earth state of mind, or paradigm, is a negative one. It constantly suggests to us that there is lack. It continually brings to our attention the negative quality of not enough of anything. Every form of communication suggests that there is a lack of everything: time, money, love, companionship, health—the list is endless. To Shift from the negative world rut, we first must Shift our personal one. We must constantly Shift our focus from lack to the focus of the Truth of omnipresent supply.

We cannot listen to what the outside senses tell us because they are only "telling us" what they "think" we want to see. They lie to us to support our beliefs. There are many examples of how the senses lie to us as they report back our current viewpoint. We cannot see things that we are not currently aware of because we see what we believe.

An example of this is the story of the landing of the Spaniards in Mexico. When the Indians saw white men standing on their shores, they thought the men were gods. The Indians had not seen them arrive, so they concluded that they must be all-powerful.

Although the Spaniards' longboats were moored within sight, the Indians had no context for such contraptions and thus did not see them. Eventually the Spaniards took the Indians out in a canoe and showed them the wake of the longboats. The Indians saw the wake, and accepted that there was something causing it that they were not seeing. After accepting the possibility that something existed that they could not see, eventually the ships became visible to them.

Emotion as magnifier.

There is a wonderful Star Trek episode where Captain Kirk and Spock and other members of the crew are trapped in what appears to be a force field. They are subjected to watching the horror of other crew members being tortured in front of them, but they are not able stop it. They cannot get out of the force field that holds them. They try every possible method to release themselves. Finally, Spock conjectures that the field is magnifying their emotions. He asks them all to stop, clear their minds, and release their emotions. Instantly they are free.

I had a memorable example of this experience. I was in the process of preparing to teach the detachment part of The Shift seminar, when my husband (at that time) and I were invited to a party. When I attend a party, I usually find myself talking to whoever finds me sitting in a corner. My ex-husband, on the other hand goes to parties and within minutes he is surrounded by a crowd.

After talking to a friend for an hour or so, I went to get something to eat, and walked past him and the usual crowd of people surrounding him.

He called me over to introduce me to the group and asked me to tell them what I did. I was immediately tongue-tied and couldn't think of how to describe it, so I explained the Star Trek story to them.

While we were talking, a large dog had been jumping up on the group with its big paws, licking everyone. The group was understandably annoyed and kept pushing him away, but he kept coming back for more.

I suggested to the group that the dog was enjoying the attention being paid to him, even if to us it was negative attention, and that this was very much like the Star Trek episode.

The emotion of annoyance was keeping the dog around. Just for fun, I asked them to stop thinking about the dog at the count of three. They agreed.

I counted, and immediately, within a split second, the dog's head flew up and he literally ran from the group. We watched him go, in awe. Even I did not expect such an immediate and dramatic result.

How does this apply to our lives? Emotion magnifies whatever we perceive as reality. Keep emotion only on what we want to reproduce—good—and we will find we are already in Heaven.

How to leave a rut.

Sit down before fact like a little child, and be prepared to give up every preconceived notion, follow humbly wherever and to whatever abyss Nature leads, or you shall learn nothing.
—T.H. Huxley

The first problem for all of us, men and women, is not to learn, but to unlearn.
—Gloria Steinem

The first step in leaving a rut is *Being Willing* to accept that there is more to life than the life we are living.

The second step in leaving a rut is to *Become Aware* of the rut. We all are in some kind of rut. Some ruts are deeper than others, but until we are all living limitless lives in every area of life, we are still in a rut somewhere.

The third step out of the rut is to understand that no matter how good life is now, it is not as good as it gets.

To Shift a point of view, return to a childlike mind. Watch young children who have been surrounded by love. These children are free of ruts. They are not thinking, "This is how it is." To them all things are new and open to possibility. They are not worried about changing their point of view because they would lose too much or appear too foolish. They don't think, "I am not supposed to do this". All they are doing is living in the moment and gaining understanding. Children do not filter information—they entertain possibilities.

What we perceive to be reality magnifies.

Before we can go anywhere, we need to know our starting point. Self-truth is the first truth. Since we are the dreamers dreaming the dream, or the mapmakers making the map, it is wise to know who we think we are. If we can't tell the truth to ourselves, how can we know Truth?

Take a moment and write down who you believe yourself to be. What are you thinking? What are you feeling? Who and what is in your life now? How do you feel about each of these people, places, and things? Tell the truth—it is the first step to freedom—but please don't attach any significance to these things. They are simply a set of beliefs.

Who am I today?
What am I thinking?
What am I feeling?
Who is in my life now?
How do I feel about each of these people?
What work am I doing?
How do I feel about this work?

OK. Now that you have told the truth, as you know it today, you can begin to know and understand yourself and what appear to be your problems. However, first let's take a look at what makes up a problem. How many times have you faced a problem with effort? We think, "If I work harder at the job, relationship, business—things will get better."

We throw our entire being into fixing the problem. And what happens? It gets worse. There is a simple reason for this. Let's go back to the beginning. What you think about and believe becomes your reality. What you perceive to be reality magnifies.

The problem has become real because each time you think of the problem, you focus on it as a problem.

Add to that the fact that the problem is never actually the problem—it is a symptom of a choice you don't remember making that is now dictating "reality." Focusing on the problem with effort magnifies it. This is because all emotion acts just like a magnifying glass. It makes bigger or more "real" whatever it is focusing on. The mind only goes along for the ride.

Some people spend years trying to remember their choices. Once they uncover them, they spend more time trying to figure out how they made them. Then they have to figure out why they made each choice. Finally, they must learn how to forgive themselves and others for the reasons for the choice. This method will work, in time.

However, there is a simpler way. It starts with knowing the Truth of who we are, and acting out of that Truth now. When we study what is Real, what is unreal becomes apparent and can be easily confronted and resolved. When we focus on what is Real, what is unreal becomes obvious.

When we focus on the unreal, what is Real remains hidden.

For example: When a bank is training its tellers to distinguish between a real or counterfeit bill it first shows them what a real one looks like. Fake bills are then obvious to them. Of course, the bank might also teach them what tricks can be used to make the bills appear real.

But first, tellers must know what real money looks like. This works in our lives too. The Bible tells us to think only on what is good, beautiful, and pure, for a good reason. We will then know what is not good, beautiful, and pure when we see it. What is not good becomes totally obvious. However, most of us have been taught to look at what doesn't work and then try to fix it! Have you noticed how hard this is?

This is not a denial of our choices, but an uncovering of them in order to choose consciously. We begin to notice the tricks that have been played on us to make something appear real when it is not. It is a process of bringing all the pieces of ourselves together. We begin to retrieve parts of our emotional self that we left behind at different levels of growth because of the choices we made.

As we begin to uncover our choices and then release any pain that they prompted, our vision clears. If we are burdened with pain from our unconscious choices, we spend much of our lives surviving. As we gather and heal our internal awareness, we are free to release the energy that was being used merely to survive, and instead we can focus that energy towards higher realms. This transforms our consciousness.

The Star Trek point of view.

Let me give you an easy way to start seeing the world differently. Pretend that you're going watch an episode of Star Trek. This is a show about a group of people who know that they are traveling on the same spaceship. They also know their mission. Their mission is to "go where no one has gone before." They even know how they are going. They are going boldly. A few minutes into the show an "it" appears. This is something that seems to be a threat, or at least a dangerous mystery.

Here's what the crew does not do. No one says, "Wow, what did we (or I) do to cause this to happen? Must be my (or your) karma catching up with me." No one blames anyone, including themselves. No one says, "Why me?" No one says, "I have such bad luck." No one judges the "it."

What they do is rally around someone on the crew who seems to have an insight into this "it." As a team, they take on the challenge. They are always willing to look for and listen to creative and insightful solutions from anyone.

What happens next? Deeper into the show the captain is faced with a decision. In some way, he must decide whether to live up to his highest understanding of what is right, or take the easier way and save the crew and/or himself. Of course, he chooses the high moral ground and that turns out to be the right answer and the "it" disappears.

Wait, there's more. What else they don't do is sit around rehashing the "it" story. What they do is play, talk, and love. Basically they have relationships.

There is one last step. It's a week later and it's time for Star Trek.

You flip on the show and what you don't see is

anyone saying, "Whoa, we better not boldly go where no one has gone before, because remember what happened last time!"

If we simply choose this Star Trek point of view, the unlimited life can begin to be ours.

We're the lid on our lives—Let's take off the lid!

Our real self is not the captive of space and time.
—W.R. Inge, Mysticism in Religion

For a number of years I taught dance classes. One of my favorite classes was for children around three years old. I never met a child at that age that didn't have rhythm. If they started class later, say after first grade, the only ones who had retained their rhythm were those who believed that it was innate to them or who never questioned their ability. If they were adults, many of the beginner dancers had totally accepted the notion that they lacked rhythm. That point of view absolutely buried the truth that their rhythm was still within. They had allowed their personal worldview to wall off, or "lid off," a basic ability.

However, even the three-year-olds would often say to me, "I can't." To counteract this I would put an empty cardboard box outside the door. I requested that they deposit any bad feelings or thoughts and the words "I can't" inside the box before they came in.

They totally understood this request and made quite an event out of dropping thoughts and words into the box. They knew that they could pick them up and have them again after class, but they never did.

I still have a memory of one little girl happily

swinging her waist- long hair as she skipped out of the room saying, "Mommy, I can do anything I want!"

Why should we put the lid on when the joy is streaming out? Saying "I can't" causes what is called a scotoma, a blind spot, which literally tells our brain not to see anything that would prove that we could.

We are all born originals—why is it so many of us die copies?
—Edward Young

Lilacs and the train.

Years ago, I experienced spring in the Eastern United States for the first time in thirty-three years. I grew up in Pennsylvania and my favorite part of spring was the lilacs blooming. I loved them for their abundance, their fragrance, their color, and the fact that they always seemed to bloom for my birthday, which is in mid-May. It had been so long since I lived in the East I was not sure what lilac bushes looked like before they had leaves. During the month of April I looked everywhere for lilac bushes. I worried because I did not see any buds on any bush that looked like a lilac to me. How would they be ready to bloom by mid-May?

The first week in May, as I sat on my front porch wondering about lilac bushes, it occurred to me that perhaps they might bloom earlier than I thought.

In less than a fraction of a second—that change of perception, that shift in point of view, that tiny thought that perhaps things were not just as I remembered, or wanted it to be—produced a huge blooming lilac bush less than fifty feet away from me.

In shock, I looked around and saw another one about 100 feet away.

What happened? Did they materialize out of thin air—or were they there all along, and it was my state of mind, my point of view, my perception of reality that totally and completely blocked the fully blooming lilac bush from my sight? You know the answer.

Here is another example. Once we lived a block from a railroad track. When the trains came through it felt and sounded like they were going directly through the house. Two trains passed through our town at night. One arrived about 12:30 a.m. and another one at 4:30 a.m. For about a month, we thought that the trains were not coming through anymore because we didn't hear them. One night, I was awake at both those times and there they were—right on time, so loud the house shook.

The trains never stopped coming through. We were what was different, not the trains. What were we? Asleep.

Seeing what is present is as simple as both of these examples. The lilacs were right in front of me and the train was still coming through. In one case, I had a point of view or paradigm—which filtered out any information about seeing blooming lilacs until mid-May. And in the other, I had a point of view that I was not awake.

Perception shifting is easy. Wake up and/or open your thought to even the smallest possibility that what you want, wish for, look for, desire, has already been provided for you, and the possibility that how you thought it was going to be might be different, and you too will look up and see what you want blooming right there—in front of you. Once you see one new idea, more will appear.

I guarantee this—I promise you this—but you must be the one who says wholeheartedly, "There is more than meets the eye, and I am willing to perceive it, now."

The only permanent solution to experiencing a different reality is to Shift and let the law of perception work on our behalf.

Things do not change; we change.
—Henry David Thoreau

No army can withstand the strength of an idea whose time has come.
—Victor Hugo

As soon as man does not take his existence for granted, but beholds it as something unfathomably mysterious, thought begins.
—Albert Schweitzer

Most people are about as happy as they make up their minds to be.
—Abraham Lincoln

SECTION TWO

The Shift To GRACIOUS

Chapter Three: The Fork In The Road

When you come to a fork in the road, take it.
—Yogi Berra

When you face a fork in the road, step on the exhilarator!
—Pat Riley

Ready—Set—Shift.

Why not change our point of view? After all, who really wants to live in a rut? We have seen that perceiving magnifies, so why not perceive something that would be more enjoyable. Here is a tool that can be used to get that "lid called you" out of the way.

The lid called you, or who you think you are, doesn't really want to change. If I am trying to accomplish something that a part of Beca is afraid of, or not ready for, or doesn't want, I have to struggle with myself.

Sometimes I am unaware that conditioned culture-impacted Beca is not in on what I want. I only find out later, when she has sabotaged me. Of course, I am now referring to myself as two people. First, there is the person called Beca who has grown up adapting and fitting into her culture or worldview. Then there is the other person to whom I have given a separate name, who is my inner core and who already knows the Truth.

I know that we all have this inner core. To help uncover it I suggest you too give yourself another name.

As you read this perhaps a name popped into your head. If one did, don't deny it. You can change it later if you want to, but use it for now even if you didn't like it. If one didn't come to you, just grab any name, and use it for now; again, you can change it later. Often you will find that name you didn't like at all will turn out to represent a strength or quality you will be proud of expressing. Write a brief history of this new name. Have fun with it. You don't have to be a human, or from this planet. What you do want is a new, broader, happier point of view for your new name.

Now that you have a new name and new history, you have a different standing point from which to view any situation. You have a vehicle that helps you to say "what if" and not be attached. You can now have a discussion with the culture-impacted you and the true you, and not attach yourself to your problem. The people who have graduated from my Shift class know how to have a discussion with another Shift Mate using the Shift name to access another point of view—with themselves and with each other. Once you find someone who enjoys this idea, exchange names, and remind each other of who you really are.

One woman reminds herself who she really is by putting her Shift name on the backside of her nameplate on her desk. Those facing her see her regular name, but she sees the name that reminds her of her true self. She uses this knowledge to expand her point of view in her day-to-day business dealings, which has resulted in a huge increase in her business and greater peace of mind.

Another woman took the name that popped into her mind, and instantly didn't like, but lived with it anyway.

One day it dawned on her that this was truly how she wanted to live her life, and now she uses it as a logo for her new business. Both of these women have pulled strength and insight from within, just by reminding themselves that they are much more than what appears on the surface.

My new name is:

My new back-story is:

Which path?

Before we can go any farther, there is a choice to be made. We have reached a crossroads with three paths. The first is the physical path. All that we have discussed up to now can be used simply to improve your physical life. The second path is the mental path. Using perception rules on this path will also improve your physical life, but will do so by improving the way that you think. The final path is the spiritual path.

Choosing this path is not a choice to improve anything but a choice to yield to the divine State of Grace and become aware of the Kingdom of Heaven within. Before you choose, consider this.

Is it possible that "this" is all a game?

And if it is a game:
• Do you know the rules?
• Do you know the purpose?
• Do you have any idea how you are doing?

Will you pretend with me for a moment? Let's call the universe, as we know it, a state of mind. The universe state of mind has a series of rules and constructs upon which we have all agreed.

The Earth is also a state of mind with its own specific rules and parameters that we have all agreed upon. This Earth state of mind is where most of us reside ninty-nine percent of the time, without knowing it is only an agreed-upon game.

The game called "Earth state of mind" is very different from all other games we play, because in other games we know we are playing a game. In this game, we have forgotten it is a game, and so we take it as a solid, for-real, this-is-the-way-it-is place.

What this Earth state of mind game has in common with all other games is that like every other game it has something to overcome, something to achieve in order to win, and rules.

In the Earth game, we must overcome the belief of lack. We must stop believing any statement that says there is not enough—of anything.

Check it out. Every one of our precepts about Earth starts with the concept "there is not enough." We all agree at least some of the time that there is not enough time, patience, resources, expertise, love, kindness, money, patience etc., don't we?

In the Earth game, there are two things we need to do in order to win—and move on—first: We must overcome the belief of lack.

Second: At the same time all (all not some) of our relationships must be harmonious and balanced. Yes it is easy to say and hard to do. But in order to "win" we must overcome the belief of lack in everything and be conscious of the abundance that is always and forever present.

This overcoming and consciousness would perfect every relationship we have. We would begin within ourselves and then branch out to family, friends, our home, our town, mankind, our world and everything in it—from our shoes to the icebergs in Antarctica.

The most difficult part of this game is that when we start with the belief that there is lack, it is hard to have perfect relationships with anything at all. Obviously to truly win the game we have to first know:
•That it is a game.
•That there is no lack.

Why is there really no lack? **Because the One Mind is not playing this game.** It—as Principle—continues to exist only as a state of continuous supply and Love. It knows nothing of the Earth game of lack we have all agreed to play. It is our perception of the game that makes the game what it is in every moment. And it is our change of perception about the game that changes the results of the game. Ah—the tangled web we weave.

Since we are in the middle of pretending that there is a game called Earth state of mind we need to know the rules of the Earth game:
• Unlike the show Survivor, in this game there is no final winner. In fact, if you are the only one left, you lose.

In this game of survival, all must survive in order for you to win.

- You must participate. Sitting on the sidelines saying, "I don't want to play" won't get you anywhere—it just delays the inevitable.
- The only way out of the game is to play.
- You can win only when you play as yourself—not pretending to be what you are not, or hiding what you are. Therefore, part of the game is discovering your unique expression and living it.
- In order to win you have to assist as many people as possible to win with you.
- There can be no desire to be or create a loser. However, some people will make a choice to be a loser until the next round.
- You cannot change another person's choice to lose.
- You must keep an open door in case the person wants to play again to win.
- You can't play for anyone; you can't take anyone's place.
- You can never drag people to the finish line, but you can encourage them to keep going.
- You must be able to recognize and walk away from those whose only goal is to keep anyone—even the person you like the least—from winning.
- You must learn to protect yourself and those you love in a way that does not harm others.
- You must always take the "good of the whole" into account, but at the same time, be true to yourself.
- All alliances are to be made for the good of all, not for the alliance.
- No action can ever be made in retaliation, or revenge. Wars do not work—any kind, any size—ever. To

win, you must find a better way.

• Accumulating anything and then not being willing to let go does not win points: It only slows you down.

The best players:

• Know the rules.

• Play by the rules.

• Spend time becoming aware of who they (and everyone else) really are, and use that perception to Shift the game.

• Trust that the more they play well the more they will remember who they are outside the game.

• Understand that sometimes what looks like losing is in reality winning.

• Know that when they understand that there is no lack, the rules are obvious and easy to follow.

• Walk their talk.

In the Earth game, the good do finish first and the bad…well sometimes we—and they—think they have won. However, look at their relationships, which is the whole point of the Earth game. You know—game over, you lose—now do it again. Or game over—you win—you can move up and on. You choose.

What do you get "here" if you win? This is the good part. Here in this Earth game you will always be wealthy, to your taste, just as you want it to be. Not because that is what you have chosen to be, but because your perception will have shifted to see that you are. You will always be at peace with your decisions and you will always feel loved.

But best of all: You will know it is a game, and you will have experienced, even if for only a moment, the door opening to an abundant Truth that no one can ever take away from you.

In addition, you may find you never have to play a state-of-mind game again.

However, if you do, it will be even more fun than the one you are playing now.

I know we were just pretending, but consider this, what if it is true? Which path will you take? I am hoping you will choose the road less traveled—the Spiritual path of Grace.

Take the lonelier path.

Two roads diverged in a wood, and I—I took the one less traveled by, And that has made all the difference.
—Robert Frost, The Road Not Taken

What is the road less traveled? Perhaps Robert Frost was referring to the path that most of us think is the lonelier path. It would appear lonelier because the majority of the people are not on this path. Very few choose the Spiritual path of Grace. On this path what used to be important drops away. At first, this may indeed seem a lonely place. Stay on the path long enough and countless abundance appears; and what dropped away will be replaced ten-fold.

In order to stay on the Spiritual path of Grace we must choose to live our highest understanding of what is moral and right. As we become more aware of Spiritual Truth our understanding of what is moral and right evolves.

However, it's easy to continue doing something even after we know it to be wrong, because we haven't gotten around to realizing that it no longer meets our standards. The less-traveled path asks us to answer to the call of

Spirit and not the siren call of small r reality.

Habits can, and will, keep us doing something that no longer serves our well-being. We must be ever-vigilant and alert as our understanding unfolds.

For those of us who have based our entire life on a certain point of view it can be even harder to relinquish it. In fact, the more successful we are at promoting our point of view, the larger our following, the more humbleness on our part is necessary to leave what we now know to be a limited point of view and Shift to Living in Grace. Our entire lives as we know them may drop away from us. It takes faith, a choice of willingness, to make this step. The path of Grace is not the easy path. It requires a great deal of us. Nevertheless, eventually we will all have to choose this one. Why not now?

To believe in the things you see and touch is no belief at all; but to believe in the unseen is a triumph and a blessing.
—Abraham Lincoln

Heaven—Harmony—Balance—Boring? Not.

Mark Twain once said that he wasn't interested in going to Heaven. After all, how could it be Heaven if he couldn't do the things that were fun to him here on Earth? Exactly. The same sentiment is found in all of us whether we are aware of it or not.

In my mid-twenties, I started telling anyone who was within two feet of me about God and Heaven. I was a "new convert" to the principles of One Mind and perfection. I talked and talked and people balked and balked. What didn't they like? The idea of perfection. Yuck. Perfection is boring. Where is the fun? Where is the drama? Where is the excitement?

I was stunned into silence and thought, "How could perfection be boring?" Two words that often describe Heaven are balance and harmony. Are these two states boring?

Harmony is the fullness of many notes blended in infinite ways to produce unlimited variations of sound. One note alone is not harmony. Harmony takes many different forms, but it is not boring.

Balance is not static. Anyone who has ever tried to balance knows that hundreds of little muscles in the body move constantly to produce what looks like a still point. Balance is not boring.

Webster's dictionary defines heaven as "A state or place of complete happiness or perfect rest attained by the good after death; the state or place of perfect union with God; any place of great beauty and pleasure; a state of great happiness…"

Does this mean we have to die to reach Heaven? Yes and no. And this may be the reason for our resistance to Heaven here and now. It is not that we think it is boring, we think we will have to change to "get there." Absolutely—we have to change.

It is easier to resist Heaven because we think it is boring than to resist Heaven because it is demanding. To be in Eden, paradise, nirvana, heaven, the Promised Land, Shangri-la—any place of complete bliss and delight and peace—we have to give up preconceived notions about what is harmony or bliss. We have to yield to the Divine Ego. We must grow.

I planted morning glories outside my porch and watched as the tendrils searched for places to twine.

I was constantly untwisting the branches as they twined in onto themselves because I had neglected to make enough places for them grow. As I untwisted, I reflected that it is the morning glories' nature to twine. Nothing will stop the irresistible movement of that drive.

Our nature is to twine too, to grow outward, express ourselves, and bloom. But, we often neglect to provide a place to grow; or where we are growing is too weak to hold our weight. We will then twine back into ourselves, and call it anger, boredom, depression, rebellion. To bloom and grow as intended we must provide the structure of Truth.

Just as our understanding of musical harmony improves with study—so does our understanding of spiritual harmony. As we become more aware of God, what we consider to be fun changes. We will have to change. We will have to die to what we used to think was harmony and is now discord.

In balance, what is still is the mind. Once I visited my parents' gym and tried out a piece of equipment that required balance. As I stepped onto the equipment my mom said, "Keep your mind still." If we keep our mind still in what we know as Heaven—the awareness of our beingness in One Mind—we always have balance.

It is easy to be in Heaven. We are already here. "The Kingdom of Heaven is within." What can feel hard is being conscious of it, acknowledging, and living it. It can seem hard to give up what we already know not to be harmony. But it is only hard if we hold onto a limited boring sense of perfection. This perfection is the one that we think we have to produce, be responsible for, and keep in place.

This perfection is really personal ego and the limited sense of self; hanging on hoping it doesn't have to die.

Supreme happiness is different for each of us at different times of our lives. Like balance, Heaven is not static. What Heaven demands of us is the willingness to die. Not die as the physical death of the body, but the death of a point of view—actually many points of view—all of them limited and ego-driven. The word perfection implies movement and all that would be necessary for us to consider something perfect. Nothing about perfection is boring.

Give up personal ego for the One Ego, become conscious of only Love and in less than a moment Heaven appears. Bliss is defined in Buddhism or Hinduism as a "state of blissful peace and harmony beyond the suffering and passions of individual existence; a state of oneness with eternal Spirit." Since the eternal Spirit is God, and God is All and the only creator, power, movement, growth, joy, fun, activity—and we are that expression of all that God is—then can Heaven be boring? No!

All are called, few have chosen.

I know I have misquoted the Bible. It really says, "For many are called, but few are chosen." (Matthew 22:14) I never could get behind that statement. To me a God operating as a Principle of Infinite Love cannot help but leave the door open to everyone. Love will always pour out Love. The sun is a wonderful example of this kind of Love. When the sun shines, it shines on us all without exception. Even when it is hidden from us it is still shining.

There is no judgment as to who we are or where we live. It doesn't change the quality of its sunshine either.

If you have chosen other paths in the past, as we all have, there is no need to fear choosing the path of Grace now. God as Principle knows nothing about any other path or state other than Grace. It is only our perception that we once walked the "wrong" path that keeps us from Grace. Grace is now, always has been, and always will be—waiting for us to become conscious that we have always lived in the State of Grace.

For now, in our limited perception, it looks as if we must walk a path to get to it. Like plants that bend to the sun, we yearn to choose Grace. It is up to us to answer "yes." It is totally up to you.

This is your moment of exercising your free will. You can take any path you wish. It is your choice. Just one reminder; sooner or later you and I will yield to the Divine Mind. Sooner or later we will have to choose the State of Grace. May I ask again? Why not now?

Chapter Four: The 8 Steps of GRACIOUS

The Fifth Step To Shift—Shift to Spiritual Perception.

When we chose the path of Spirituality, our point of view from that point forward must be that of Reality. There is no room for standing on both sides of the issue. Let's be clear about what we mean by Reality. Reality is Heaven here and now. Reality is the Truth that what appears to be material is really Spiritual. Reality is One—of everything. There is no separation or duality. Reality is the reflection, the thought, and the creation of One Mind. The Reality is, there was never a separate material creation.

Much of the time we have to argue attorney-style with our small-i (ego) so that it will step aside and yield to Truth. Here is the premise we are going to ask our small-i to agree to in order to walk the Spiritual path of Grace.

The Shift premise.
There is a Higher Power.
That Higher Power is Mind.
There is only One Mind.
That Mind is Infinite Intelligence.
That Mind is Perfect Love.
That Mind is the ONLY Cause and Creator.
That Mind is God and Its idea = I AM.

If you read the above and thought "religion," stop! It doesn't matter if you resisted this premise because it reminded you of religion, or if you loved it because it reminded you of religion. This is not a religious premise. Please don't place unlimited abundance within the codes and rules of religious belief. All religions have this premise at their core, but they have mostly strayed from it in order to maintain their reason for being.

If you resist knowing and accepting that there is a Higher Power, God, then perhaps you are not yet ready to live from an unlimited viewpoint, and it's still more comfortable for you to stay with your current life than to let go of limiting ideas. If so, wait to read this book when you are ready and willing. If you are willing at least to just look at the possibility, read on.

The most important part of this Shift is to desire to know and act from the understanding of what is True—and what is True is all is God. We could also use the word Good since Good and God were originally the same word. Substitute the word Good for God if it helps you to avoid any preconceived notions about God. However, when I am using the word Good instead of God, it is not the good that is the opposite of evil, which is a limited and dualistic approach. Good in this context means Perfect One.

If you are ready for an unlimited viewpoint, you know and accept that there is a Higher Power, or at least you are willing to look at the possibility. You can call this Higher Power any name you wish as long as it contains the understanding that there is only One, an Infinite Loving Intelligence. To make this point clear, I will discuss it from the standpoint that God, Higher Power, is Mind.

You can call God the One Taste, One Engineer, Love, Good, whatever registers within as True for you.

Is there a God? As a teenager, I briefly questioned this. My first taste of religion had been one where questioning was not allowed. This presented me with ideas from which I could draw no logical conclusions. It suggested that we could never understand God and were not allowed to try. It told me that I could never be good, that guilt was part of my being. I could not accept these teachings, so in tossing out the religion I also tossed out my understanding that there is a Higher Power.

This didn't last long. Simple things told me there was Something much more, in day-to-day life, guiding others and me.

It was an internal knowing. It was the blast of joy that came from seeing the clouds one day as I started down the stairs at my dorm. I glanced up and saw the sky through a skylight. It was awareness of the simple beauty of what I was looking at, and of the incredible Intelligence of what must have created it. It was the awareness that even though I thought I was painting a picture, or choreographing a dance, something higher than my human self was guiding me. I knew without question, as you do, that there is a Higher Power. There was something greater than my human self. I just didn't know how to make use of that knowledge. I wanted to know more about this Higher Power. After much reading, thinking and listening, I understood that One Mind is the only answer.

Only an Infinite Intelligent Mind could hold the world and the infinity of being in Its thought. Could there be two minds running the world? No. Even two human minds can never agree totally on everything.

It has to be One Mind, an Infinite Intelligence.

The next step in this premise is that there is only One Cause and Creator. Since there is only One Mind, there can be just one Cause, one Creator. Since there is only One power, there is no other power to create something other than perfection. This means there is nothing that we did or didn't do that could remove us from of the State of Grace, or from being the reflection of One Loving Mind. We can breathe a sigh of relief! All we need do to is yield to the State of Grace to become conscious of the Truth of One.

The radical view that we'll soon begin to live from is that there is only One Mind, One Cause, One Creator, and It is Intelligent Infinite Love. This means that perfection, joy, and good are the Truth about who we are. The Truth is not some goal to achieve or someplace to go. When we make this kingdom of God—One Mind, Love—the starting point, all other needs are met. Heaven is here, at hand, and ours now, because it is Truth. We can live on Main Street and still be living in Heaven, because there is only One Creation, God's, and that One is Spiritual. This is our Spiritual point of view.

Love's Promise—The Spiritual Laws of Grace.

1. But, seek ye first the kingdom of God, and his righteousness; and all these things shall be added unto thee.
  —Matthew 6:33, Bible
2. Ask, and it shall be given you; seek, and ye shall find; knock, and it shall be opened unto you.
  —Matthew 7:7, Bible
3. And it shall come to pass, that before they call, I will answer.
  —Isaiah 65:24, Bible

Let's look at the Laws that must proceed from the fact that there is only One Mind, One Infinite Loving Intelligence.

Although many have taught us how to step on the road to freedom, and many books guide us there, the Bible is one book that has stated clearly the universal Laws. And it was Christ Jesus who fully interpreted these laws for us and demonstrated that they come from the One Mind, which is Love. Following these laws, we can understand how and why Shifting works.

These are real Laws. These are not laws as we often think of laws, which can be negotiated, or side-stepped by a spin on the circumstances. These Laws cannot be put aside even for a moment. These are the Laws that set the ground of our being and cannot be anything but true in every moment.

Let's start with the **First Spiritual Law.** "Seek ye first the kingdom of God, and his righteousness; and all these things shall be added unto thee." This is the most important Law of all because it is the underlying Truth supporting the rest of the Laws.

Seek—what does that mean? It is an active statement. Seek means go after, strive, learn about, test, try on, use, get, know. Don't just wait, hope, or dream—seek. Who seeks? We do. We cannot ask someone else to seek (see) for us. We must find the awareness and understanding within. Our salvation, awareness, does not rest on another's work, but on our own. Of course, we use others' wisdom to guide us but we must live Truth ourselves. In the end, seeking becomes seeing what is True and resting in that knowledge. We are not seeking to find God. After all, we have never been separated from It. We are seeking to be conscious of God.

How do we seek? First. Not after we take care of everything else. Not after we have tried every other method to accomplish something. No. First we seek. What do we seek? Ah, the kingdom of God. What is the kingdom of God? It is the complete awareness and consciousness of One God. It is Truth. It is Heaven. We are seeking the absolute reign and habitation of God, the kingdom of Love. We are seeking the place where there are no limitations or filters from any paradigm. Libraries are filled with sages' attempts at answering the question, "What is the kingdom of God?" But let us gather all that knowledge together for ourselves, follow the guidance of the Christ consciousness, and call the kingdom of God that which is all-loving, truthful, available, complete, perfect, continuous, absolute, omnipotent, omniscient, omnipresent, omniaction—One.

We seek this state of being, the Divine state of Being—and what happens? In the state of consciousness we call "life on Earth," what we need becomes visible to us. The action we take in the world is to seek first what is Truth and the rest will follow. Just as surely as a wake follows a boat, what we desire to see follows our understanding God First.

The Second Spiritual Law says—"Ask, and it shall be given you; seek, and ye shall find; knock, and it shall be opened unto you." This is again an active state. However, it is primarily a promise. If we ask, it will be given. If we seek, we will find. It is the motive that counts. Our motive must be to seek Truth. Our motive is to integrate what we know about Truth into our daily active lives, not to get things. We must live the Truth. We cannot just keep the knowledge behind a wall, using it only as a periodic catharsis to feel close to God.

We must keep God within all our actions. If we do this, when we knock, we will see the already open door.

The Third Spiritual Law is perhaps the most comforting. "Before they call, I will answer." Wow! This means before I even know I need something; it is already prepared for me. It's like being hungry and thinking, "When I get home I'll have to make some food," and when you arrive, someone has already prepared a wonderful meal, ready for you just to sit down and partake. This is the continuous blessing being given to us.

Expect ease and simplicity.

Early in life, we begin to believe that if things are hard to do, that is good. We are told to value hard work, so if it came to us easily its value was less. Is this what we wish for our children? As we hold them in our arms the first year of their lives do we look upon them with love and think, "I wish for you hard work and labor?"

Could an Infinite Loving One, the essence of Father-Mother Love, even think this thought? No. A Principle of Love does not know an opposite of Itself. Love would wish for us more than we can ever wish for ourselves, or for those we love. It goes even farther than that. Love does not "wish" for anything because Love is infinite supply, and Its individual expressions (you and me) are expressions of that supply.

As we express the activity of Love (One Mind), we will find that all is easy and simple, but probably not comfortable. In our human minds, we believe that uncomfortable is hard. But it doesn't have to be.

Since we are still appearing to live in the rut of thinking we're separate from God, we may experience discomfort as we step out of that rut. This discomfort is not Mind imposed or Mind wished; it's our holding on to old points of view. The faster we relinquish our belief that we are separate from God the less discomfort we'll feel. Simple does not mean that we don't have actions to take and things to learn. However, we'll be able to measure our understanding of alignment and harmony with the One Mind (Love) by the ease and simplicity that greets us as we live our lives. Remember, "Before you call, I will answer" is a Law of Life. All we are doing is shifting our point of view to the One Loving Mind, and as we do, that which has already been created will appear. Once again, we are choosing the path of Spirituality. We choose to live from the point of view of Reality and the State of Grace.

We are not creators or co-creators.

Since there is only Mind, there is only one Creator. However, in this New Age world we are often spoken of as co-creators and creators. Can this be true? Are we actually co-creators? No! God knows nothing of a life that is less than perfection, so It could not co-create an imperfect life. In that sense, we are not co-creators. We are also not co-creators in the Reality of One Perfect Love. We are reflection, thinking, and expression, of the One Mind, not co-creators.

Are we creators? Have we created the situations that we find ourselves in, the life we live? The answer is yes— in the sense that we do experience a life that is based on our point of view.

It is our perception that determines our reality, so in that way we are creators; but again not co-creators since God does not know of imperfection. Our thoughts and words manifest into what appears as something outside. This is the mental world. As we awaken to our true heritage, that this is a Spiritual world, then what appears outside becomes more as God knows it to be.

Guilt and fear only serve to make any problems we experience more real. Emotion does magnify what we perceive to be reality. Emotions such as guilt and fear keep the problem real and personal. We do not attach a reason or purpose to the "its" that appear in our lives. Some "its" appear because the worldview has such a strong belief in the reality of the "its."

As in the Star Trek point of view, we must confront and dissolve any "its" that appear. We do this by knowing the Truth, not by feeling and living in guilt and fear. It helps to remember that if what we are seeing is not perfect, then it is only a belief, an illusion, and it can and will dissolve immediately when we step into Truth, just as the darkness dissolves when we turn on the light.

It is important to remember that nothing will ever harm our True being. No matter what the external picture may be, we are always safe in Love. It is how we approach the "its" in our thoughts that give them power. Relax. Know that all we have to do is Shift to Living in Grace.

GRACIOUS Perception Rules.

But how do we stay in the Spiritual point of view all the time? We know now that what we perceive as reality magnifies to produce more of the same.

We know that we become conscious of the unlimited Reality by Shifting our point of view. But, how do we Shift our thinking? In the middle of a belief of problem or lack, how do we get back to Grace? Sometimes we are aware of Grace without any effort on our part, as Love takes over. Other times we have to "talk ourselves into it." The GRACIOUS steps are designed for just those times.

For the next eight chapters we'll look at eight steps we can use to remain aware and awake, to uncover and dissolve the beliefs that are creating a limited reality, and to stay conscious of the State of Grace.

Follow the path of the unsafe, independent thinker. Expose your ideas to the dangers of controversy. Speak your mind and fear less the label of 'crackpot' than the stigma of conformity. And on issues that seem important to you, stand up and be counted at any cost.
—Thomas J. Watson

What we think determines what we are and do, and conversely, what we are and do determines what we think.
—Aldous Huxley

All that we are is the result of what we have thought: it is founded on our thoughts, it is made up of our thoughts.
—Dhammapada

After years of probing the spectacular mysteries of the Universe, I have been led to a firm belief in the existence of God. The grandeur of the cosmos serves only to confirm my beliefs in the certainty of a creator. I just cannot envision this whole Universe coming into being without something like divine will. The natural laws of the Universe are so precise that we have no difficulty building a space ship to fly to the moon and can time the flight with the precision of a fraction of a second.

—Werner Von Braun

Chapter Five: G: God First

Our goal is purity.

Hold thought steadfastly to the enduring, the good, and the true, and you will bring these into your experience proportionally to their occupancy of your thoughts.
—Mary Baker Eddy, Science and Health with Key to the Scriptures

Finally, brethren, whatsoever things are true, whatsoever things are honest, whatsoever things are just, whatsoever things are pure, whatsoever things are lovely, whatsoever things are of good report, if there be any virtue, and if there be any praise, think on these things.
—Philippians 4:8, Bible

Be pure. What a concept; one I was sure I could never live up to. But when I learned that the original meaning of the word pure was "freedom from improper views" I began to believe it was something I might accomplish. I found I could change my improper views as soon as I was clear on what was meant by "improper."

The most basic improper view is that we are separate, that Spirit or God has to come to us—rather than that we are an inseparable part of Spirit. Eliminate this view and we can begin to live our lives knowing that Heaven is normal and that we are already there.

Good, true, beautiful, and pure.

How do we put God First? To begin, we must see and live with only God, in action. This means that we must focus our thought only on what is good, true, beautiful, and pure. This may feel impossible because our habit is to focus on the negative.

Dr. Albert Ellis, an early advocate of cognitive therapy, said that we walk around with about 5,000 distorted ideas about ourselves. This means we may have about 50,000 negative thoughts a day! Remember the Earth game (or small r reality) claims there is not enough. We have the habit of seeing what does not work, which is the absence of Truth.

With this habit of seeing the negative first, it may appear difficult to change our focus. However, it will be easy if we just remember who we are. Shifting is not a process of becoming someone else who can focus on the good, the true, and the beautiful; it's remembering that we are the expression of God. In other words, all we ever have been in Reality is the expression of good, true, beautiful, and pure. We must stop identifying with what we are not, and start knowing and living from the Truth of who we are.

Putting God First means consistently asking ourselves: "How does God 'see' this person, place, or thing?" Given we are still operating, for the most part, within our human mind; we must come up with ways to use that mind to awaken us to God. One way we can accomplish this is to practice translating things back into thoughts.

Remember, what we think becomes our reality.

Therefore, what looks like a thing "out there" is really just our thought "in here" appearing as a solid object in our so-called material world.

So let's start at the beginning, with thought—and translate these things back to their true origin, into qualities of God. Once we learn how to do this, we will begin to live as part of the wealth and abundance that is Truth.

Thoughts are things.

Gradually philosophers and scientists arrived at the startling conclusion that since every object is simply the sum of its qualities, and since qualities exist only in the mind, the whole objective universe of matter and energy, atoms and stars, does not exist except as a construction of the consciousness, and edifice of conventional symbols shaped by the senses of man.
—Lincoln Barnett, The Universe and Dr. Einstein

Whatever we think becomes a thing. Rather than deal with the thing (effect), let us deal with the thought (cause). Once we really understand this, anything will always be available to us. However, our goal is not things—it is Truth. That is why the First Spiritual Law is "Seek ye first the kingdom of God, and his righteousness, and all these things shall be added unto you."

The way we learn how to understand things as thoughts is to translate the thing back to its qualities. What we are learning to do is translate what we think we need back into thought.

We begin to look for the qualities or value of the "thing."

Qualities are descriptions of true substance and can be stated in one or two words—such as love, integrity, kindness, grace, gentleness, peace, happiness, luxury, joy, and so on. Living in our ruts, we think we want the "thing."

We sacrifice all qualities of true wealth in our lives to accumulate "things." We forget that we work to express the qualities of who we are. In this forgetting, we often sacrifice the quality of time with family or the peace of mind to get the money to buy a thing that we think will provide this for us. Once we begin to see true wealth as a quality we will see that we're drowning in wealth, we just haven't learned yet how to drink it. Our true nature is always available to us. It does not depend on how much we know, but on the quality of our thought.

PRACTICAL GOD FIRST.

Turning things into thoughts.

Pick anything that you're thinking about or desiring to see and list its qualities. For example, let's say that you were thinking about a car. You want the idea or quality of transportation. So how would you like that transportation to look? You might say that its qualities include safety, effortlessness, speed, security, luxury, grace, convenience, and so on.

You have probably phrased this request as something you want or need. However, if you use the words "need" or "want," they imply that you're lacking something. It is a statement of separation. As an expression or reflection of the Infinite One Loving Mind, how could you lack? If you believe that you are lacking, you are.

What we perceive to be reality magnifies, so if we perceive lack, we receive lack. An unlimited Reality cannot lack; therefore neither can you.

You have never been separate from God. In addition, wanting something often involves our ego, or human will asking for it. When we use human will, or ego, we are walking the mental or physical path. We think we are the cause and creator. We believe that if we do enough, know enough, or work hard enough, we can fix the problem. This is not putting God First. It is putting "me first." To avoid this trap of personal ego, which blinds us to the will of God, we ask instead "to see." Since everything has already been created, we are asking ourselves to wake up to what has already been provided.

Steps to making qualities lists.

Remember again we are not interested in things here. We are interested in knowing God. Since things are in essence composed of qualities, we translate back into qualities the things of which we desire to become conscious.

Step 1: Take a moment and list 8–10 qualities of something you want to "see". Use one word to express each quality. If you are using sentences, you have not come to the heart or essence of it.

Step 2: There are two kinds of qualities lists: You can either list the qualities of the thing itself, or you can list the qualities of how you will feel when you have it.

For example, let's go back to the idea of buying a car. Your quality list for the thing—or car—might contain ideas such as red, fast, inexpensive, safe, etc.

If you choose to do a qualities list of how you will feel when you drive this car, it might read "wealthy, secure, free, joyful, etc."

If you wish, do both lists. Otherwise, do the list that makes the most sense to you. What you choose to see does not matter, it can be as important as having a home or as simple as setting the table for dinner. It is being conscious of the qualities of these "things" that makes a difference.

Step 3: Now that you have the qualities list, the next step is to put these qualities in order.

Why is this important? Have you ever been at a place in your life where nothing happens towards what you want no matter what you do? This is probably because you have a quality or value block. If you have two values that feel equal to you, your core-self will be confused as to which one to provide. Continuing with the car example, let's say you list both the qualities of luxury and frugal. Until you know which quality is first, you'll be stuck and nothing will happen. This is because at first glance they appear to be conflicting. However, once your list is in order you can receive, or become conscious of, all of what you have listed. In an unlimited reality, all has been provided for you already under the law of God's Grace.

You need help to put the list in order. Have someone else take your list and help you. Don't look at your list while this person is working with you, as this will engage brain and logic. What we want to engage is your heart and inspiration.

The person with your list will ask you the following question: "**Which is more important to you**" and will give you two words on the list to compare.

The person must not give you any other verbal or physical cues. Don't listen to anything except your inner voice, and give the answer it tells you. Don't argue with it. If you are unable to choose one as more important than the other, the person should ask you, "**Which one can you not live without?**"

Notice that your mind tells you that if you choose one you might not get the other. This is coming from the point of view that there is never enough and that you don't deserve everything you want. Since neither statement is true, just notice these thoughts and move on.

The truth is, once you are clear about what you desire to see, you will be able to see and receive all these qualities. Each word must be compared with every word until you have an ordered list. You will probably be surprised at the order if you have stayed with your heart and trusted your answers.

WORKSHEET FOR QUALITIES LISTS

I desire to be conscious of: _____

These are the qualities of how it "looks"—after putting the list in order:

1. _____
2. _____
3. _____
4. _____
5. _____
6. _____
7. _____
8. _____

These are the qualities of how I will feel—after putting the list in order:

1. _____
2. _____
3. _____
4. _____
5. _____
6. _____
7. _____
8. _____

Now that you have a list, how do you use it?

1. Use the qualities as a filter.

If something appears that you think might be what you are looking for and does not have at least the first four qualities—with the first one first, it is not "it." Think of the time you will save if you can eliminate quickly and easily what is not right for you.

For example, if you find that safety is first on your quality list for a means of transportation and the car you are looking at has a very low safety record, don't buy this car no matter how much you love it. If you buy it, you will eventually be unhappy with it, and somehow you will unconsciously figure out how to get rid of it.

2. See the qualities everywhere.

See the qualities in everything, not just in what you're seeking. Notice that they're always with you in many forms. You have always had and always will have each quality on your list if you just look.

A quality does not have to belong to you. It can appear anywhere. All of what you see is already yours because you can see it. The goal is to notice that the quality you're looking for in an object already exists everywhere, and since you can see it—it exists for you—now.

3. Be grateful for each quality as you see it.

Be grateful for these qualities each time you see them, no matter where they occur.

If the person you dislike most has one of these qualities, be grateful that you have seen this quality in your life. Know that if it is "out there" it was first "within here" and therefore always available.

4. Be and live these qualities yourself.

Now that you have begun to live with God First, no longer is having the "thing" you wanted so important. You have discovered that it already exists as God's thoughts—qualities.

As we express gratitude, we are Living in Grace. The result? Sometimes we realize we don't actually need the thing we were asking to see, or it turns up in another package, or it appears in a way greater than we could have dreamed.

Whichever way this happens, we have begun with seeking the kingdom of God first. That beginning cannot help but produce in our world whatever we need at the moment, because we began with the correct premise. We become conscious of always having whatever we need. We have never been abandoned, nor could we ever be. Looking for qualities opens your eyes to what has always been and always will be yours.

To believe in God for me is to feel that there is a God, not a dead one, or a stuffed one, but a living one, who with irresistible force urges us toward more loving.
—Vincent Van Gogh

Happiness is when what you think, what you say, and what you do are in harmony.
—Mahatma Gandhi

A human being is a part of the whole called by us universe, a part limited in time and space. He experiences himself, his thoughts and feelings as something separated from the rest, a kind of optical delusion of his consciousness. This delusion is a kind of prison for us, restricting us to our personal desires and to affection for a few persons nearest to us. Our task must be to free ourselves from this prison by widening our circle of compassion to embrace all living creatures and the whole of nature in its beauty.

—Albert Einstein

Chapter Six: R: Repent

Repent: *Original meaning: Change completely the way you think. Or: Turn around and walk the other way.*

Repent [i.e., change completely the way you think: Shift] for the kingdom of God is at hand.
—Matthew 3:2, Bible

Christ Jesus asked us to "repent for the kingdom of God is at hand." The meaning of this phrase becomes clearer when we use the original meaning of the word—"to change completely the way you think, or turn around and walk the other way".

Lew Sterrett of Miracle Mountain Ranch gives a most unusual and memorable demonstration of the State of Grace and the meaning of repent. He illustrates his points while training a horse. It makes no difference if you know nothing about horses (I don't) or everything about horses; the message is clear to those who are willing to accept it.

As Lew begins to work with a horse it becomes evident that the horse thinks he knows what is good for him far better than Lew. He resists any and all demands made upon him. Fear blinds the horse to seeing the possibilities that could be available to him by simply yielding.

As Lew continues to demand the horse's attention using boundaries and love, the horse responds with anger, aggression, pouting, and stubbornness, not caring if he hurts anyone, including himself, in the process.

Does this sound like what we do when Truth asks us to repent and change our point of view?

As Lew continues to hold to the demands he has made and apply love, the horse eventually learns that bowing his head in humility to his master's desire gives him more freedom than he could ever acquire on his own.

What the horse has done is repent—seen things differently and yielded his personal ego. It is important to note that the horse could not have achieved this state of mind on his own. He needed a "trainer" to assist him in yielding his personal point of view. Our human minds are like the horse. The human mind can never get to the State of Grace on its own. It needs Truth to apply pressure and boundaries.

The amount of time it took and how uncomfortable the lesson was depended entirely upon the horse's attachment to how he wanted things to remain and the level of his unwillingness to yield.

We respond in the same way to God's boundaries and Love. We believe we are the creators and that we know more than God. We are afraid to yield to God who is our Master. Our trust is with the material world and what we can do to manipulate it to our advantage.

Lew knew the fullness of the horse's potential and demanded it of him. He did not enable the horse to stay in a resistant frame of mind because of fear he wouldn't be liked.

He held the standard of the truth of the horse for the horse—until the horse learned it for himself. In humility, the horse came to the State of Grace. The peace and joy that resulted from this yielding was tangible to all who watched.

The State of Grace.

The law was given by Moses, but grace and truth came by Christ Jesus.
—John 1:17, Bible

Moses brought us laws to follow so we could be good, wise, and loving humans. Christ Jesus brought us the Laws of Grace. Living from the State of Grace, we can understand the laws of Moses as not telling us what we shouldn't do, but what we actually couldn't do. Jesus revealed in the Sermon on the Mount (Matthew 5:1–48) that Grace is not a karmic law. The doing of "wrong" is punishment in itself. It happens because we have stepped out of the State of Grace. We act out of a misguided sense, a missed perception. God is not punishing us: God is pure Love. We have punished ourselves by believing in and acting out of separation and duality. As we become conscious of Grace, the "karmic debt" is dissolved. In the Sermon on the Mount, we are presented with the statements of how we think it is—and how it is. It is the new understanding of God that leads us to Grace.

We will find the State of Grace as we bow to the awareness that we are the expression of God, the instrument of God's will. Within the State of Grace, we will find the peace, freedom, and unlimited abundance we work so hard for, and will never receive, while believing in the material world. God's plan for us often involves us doing things we would rather not do. Since everything is a result of perception, all "problems" are a result of our point of view. It's hard to change a problem; it is easier to redirect our point of view.

Doing what we love.

I sat at a table full of successful women a few years ago. Someone asked me what I did and as usual, I struggled for an answer. After all, what was I to say? "I teach people how to transform their lives by rethinking how they view themselves and their world."

That is probably what I should have said but instead I mumbled something and settled back to listen. The talk turned to golf, and one woman asked another if she golfed. "Yes," she responded. "However, even though I keep my clubs in my car, I never seem to do that one thing I really love, which is golf." This prompted the woman next to her to ask, "Why do we do that? Why don't we do the things we love?"

At this point, I burst into the conversation and said, "That's what The Shift is about!" Instead of living lives that are only partially fulfilling and focusing on despair, anger or hurt—it Shifts our attention and our emotion to the blessings that are always surrounding us. When we repent, and use the power of perception to Shift to an expanded sense of what is possible, our life reflects the change. We find ourselves doing what we love and receiving more in life than we ever thought possible.

How did that happen?

How does it happen that we don't do what we love to do? It happens because we decided. Usually we don't remember the exact moment—but we decided not to do the things we love to do.

Decided not to trust again, decided to stop doing things that appear too difficult, decided not to believe in our dreams or decided not to do the work that really excites us.

We tell ourselves stories that go something like this:

- One time I decided to get the job I really wanted, but it made too many people unhappy so I will never do that again.
- One time I took a bus and it was so awful I will never take the bus again.
- One time I played golf and I made a fool of myself so I decided never to play golf again.
- One time I gave a speech and someone laughed so I never spoke in front of a group again.
- One time I was deeply in love and that person left me so I will never trust again.

And that is how it happens. One time—something happened that wasn't just right—and that was the end of that. Isn't that silly? What if a baby said, "One time I stood up and then I fell down so now I don't stand up anymore."

Think about it. Every decision of "I won't do that again," was made when we were younger than we are now and didn't know as much about anything as we do now. In addition, usually the decision was based on circumstances that are no longer true.

Become aware of how many things you have decided "not to do again" by paying attention to how you rationalize to yourself your decisions about not trying something. Listen carefully and you will hear yourself tell the story of the original problem.

Are you willing to live your life based on a decision you made when you were 2, 5, 10, 20, 40—or even yesterday? Couldn't we all just try again?

Example is not the main thing in influencing others. It's the only thing.
—Albert Schweitzer

My life is my message.
—Mahatma Gandhi

To try again—push on the pain.

Years ago, I wanted to learn scuba diving. I did very well. In fact, I did so well when we went out on the boat for the dive no one paid much attention to me. The instructor was busy with the others who seemed afraid. I wasn't afraid at all—until I got in the water and swam away from the boat. As I scanned where I was—in the middle of nowhere—I experienced a panic attack. It took several minutes before anyone noticed my thrashing around and helped me back to the boat.

I wanted to say, "One time I went scuba diving and it was way too scary so I will never do that again." But I didn't.

Instead, I pushed on the pain. At least once a day I would imagine myself back out in the water and I would re-experience the panic. (I was getting a lot of dental work done at the time so waiting for the dentist in the dental chair proved to be a great time to do this, but anywhere will do.)

Every time I pushed on the pain by reliving the experience, I broke out into a sweat and started shaking.

However, each time I played the scene over, the panic would subside a little bit more until one day nothing happened at all and I was able to imagine myself back out in the water actually diving and enjoying it.

I booked myself to go out with my original instructor on the next dive. It had taken me six months to feel ready, but the instructor was delighted that I was going to try again. I was still afraid, but with the guidance and support of the instructor and a friend, I made it out and back. I will never forget the feeling of elation I experienced as the rest of the dive group celebrated my personal victory.

Besides pushing on the pain, there is another principle in this story. I asked for help from someone that could and would help me—the instructor and a scuba diving friend.

One of my granddaughters was a little afraid of going in the closed slide at McDonalds. It didn't stop her though. She would approach one of the other kids who was easily going through the slide and say, "I am a little afraid, would you hold my hand?" These perfect strangers always said "yes." Wouldn't you? We can all find that someone who is not afraid of doing what we are afraid of doing and ask if that person will "hold our hand."

Learn the lesson and don't do it again.

It's never a competence problem. It's an ethical, moral crisis. It's a problem of character.
—General Norman Schwarzkopf

Sometimes we should not do it again. We should not go back to abusive relationships, not put our hand on a hot stove, not step out in front of a car.

Nevertheless, we may do that same dumb thing again if we just say, "I will never do that again" without any understanding of what happened. The whole event or choice wasn't wrong; it was a part of it that was wrong. After all, we all need to be loved, we all need to use the stove, and we all have to cross the street sometime.

Figure out which part not to do again and then never do it that way again. Decide to love again, travel again, dream again, trust again, speak again, and experience the full, abundant, and free life you were meant to live. Do this all from the understanding that you are the expression of God.

Remember: an error in the premise leads to an error in the conclusion. Start with God First and all that is like God follows.

Change the focus of your thought.

In our era, the road to holiness necessarily passes through the world of action.
—Dag Hammarskjold

A few years ago, I found myself feeling quite depressed. Although that was a common state many years ago, nowadays it's something I am surprised to find in myself.

"What started this?" I wondered. "Just a few hours ago I was filled with gratitude and joy. Now I am sad, crying, and tired."

Reminding myself that it was not a problem of being depressed but of a point of view, and that therefore I needed to repent—and redirect my thought—it occurred to me that I had just finished reading (for fun?) a romantic novel.

I had imagined that it would relax me, but instead I entered the culture of the novel and began comparing my life to it. I found myself feeling like a loser because I did not have a romantic man in my life at that moment.

What had changed? Nothing had changed but my thinking. My thought before was focused on feeling free and happy and full of individuality. Now I was focused on what I didn't seem to have—note the word seem—in my world.

At a friend's prompting, I refocused on who I really am, Spirit. I reminded myself that I am always loved and loving, and never lacking. The depression vanished, and joy flooded in to fill the space.

What happened here? I repented. Most of us think that to repent means that we have been bad and must pay for our sins. However, let's look at what the word sin really means.

It means, "missing the mark." I had certainly missed the mark by focusing on a cultural paradigm that did not include the love I was already experiencing. This was not the book's fault, but my own in the way I was thinking about my life. I was missing the mark. I was sinning.

While I was sinning, I was depressed. In essence, I was paying for my sin. As long as I thought that way, I was unhappy. Therefore, I repented. Since the word repent means "change completely the way you think," isn't this the same as Shifting? Once we notice the sin, or the missed mark, we can immediately move to Truth.

Mary Baker Eddy said, "The belief in sin is punished so long as the belief lasts."

I Shifted my thought to Spiritual Reality. I was no longer missing the mark. I was no longer suffering.

Revolution in thought is the only revolution.

For any change to be real it must be radical or, using the original meaning of the word—it must be a root change. We cannot pile good thoughts on top of limited beliefs and expect that this will be enough. We must have a revolution in thought. This revolution is based on the following root position: that God is all. Thus, we completely change the way we think. It is not enough merely to state, "God is all." Unless we back this statement with action and understanding, it is simply wishful or magical thinking.

The Shift to Living in Grace requires more than lip service. It is a conscious, constant awareness of God as the only One.

Always Back to One.

And verily I say unto you, that whosoever shall say unto this mountain, Be thou removed and be thou cast into the sea; and shall not doubt in his heart, but shall believe that those things which he saith shall come to pass; he shall have whatsoever he saith: Therefore I say unto you, what things so ever ye desire, when ye pray, believe that ye shall receive them, and ye shall have them.
—Mark 11:23, Bible

No matter what the situation, in order to see the Truth of it, we must return to knowing only One God.

During the shooting of a movie, when the director wants to run a scene again, the director says "Back to one" and the entire cast and crew go back to where they were originally placed. We must say in every situation— Back to One—One Mind, One Cause, One Creator and Creation, which is Love. In doing this, we are starting from the correct premise.

In *Science and Health: With Key to the Scriptures,* Mary Baker Eddy gives us seven names for God that state God's qualities. She names God as Life, Truth, Love, Principle, Spirit, Soul, and Mind. Each name can fit a particular occasion as we apply the principle of Back to One.

For example: Many years ago, I was faced with a horrible situation. I had left the father of my three children, and in retaliation, he "kidnapped" them and took them to back to where we had grown up. I was lucky; I knew where they were. Even so, the pain of losing them was almost unbearable. I was also dealing with the trauma of leaving him, even though it was necessary.

I asked my dearest and closest friends not to let me return to that situation, as I woke every night in the middle of a nightmare thinking that I would slip and go back to him, if only to have my children again. I also had just begun a full load at college, ten years older than everyone else, as a student in the dance department.

In this state of mind, I was fairly incapable of functioning other than at a basic survival level. To understand God at that time seemed beyond my capability.

What I could grasp was the word Principle. Since God is Love and Principle, nothing but a loving result would emerge for my children and me.

I did not try to visualize the outcome. I did not "tell God" how I wanted it to be. I attempted to stay in the consciousness that God, Love was all that was present, and the result would bless everyone. The result, in spite of all predictions to the contrary and reports that it would be impossible: I was granted custody of all three children—in both states! My daughters returned home with me. My son chose to stay with his dad, as he felt this was the loving thing to do.

I will never forget the feeling of seeing my children again (over nine months had gone by) and the gratitude I felt knowing that, with just a small understanding of Principle, this wonderful result could occur. What had I done? I had Shifted my point of view from a fear-based, limited, lack producing, and small r reality and focused on the qualities of Principle, the qualities of Truth.

I yielded my personal ego. I chose instead to witness the Truth that there is only One Mind. The word Principle was fitting for me on this occasion because I had to continue to remind myself that Truth was fair and loving and consistent. I chose to not outline the outcome, as much as I wanted my children returned to me. I did my best not to be governed by fear, anger, and revenge, but instead by understanding and love. This Shift brought me in alignment with God—and that alignment produced an outward result that benefited everyone concerned.

The biblical saying that, if you have faith the size of a grain of mustard seed you can move a mountain was true for me, and it is true for you.

PRACTICAL REPENT.

When I was a kid, I used to think that if I cleaned my room every Saturday morning and went to confession right after that, my repenting was done for the week. Now that I know repenting means to shift the way I think, it takes a lot more diligence on my part!

Here is a great way to stay on track—all day, every day: Ponder one of God's names throughout the day. Look for the qualities in evidence each day that represent that particular name. For example: for the name Mind you might see the evidence, or qualities, of order, intelligence, and perfect placement. You get the idea!

Here is a list that you could ponder for each day of the week.

Monday—Mind
Tuesday—Spirit
Wednesday—Principle
Thursday—Soul
Friday—Life
Saturday—Truth
Sunday—Love

Make notes in a journal about what you learn. Pay particular attention to the fact that as you see the qualities of the name and are grateful that these qualities are in your life now, you'll experience even more of each, in a variety of ways.

We must love one another as God loves each one of us. To be able to love, we need a clean heart. Prayer is what gives us a clean heart. The fruit of prayer is a deepening of faith and the fruit of faith is love. The fruit of love is service, which is compassion in action.
—Mother Teresa

You might as well not be alive if you're not in awe of God.
—Albert Einstein

True religion is the life we lead, not the creed we profess.
—Louis Nizer

The various religions are like different roads converging on the same point. What difference does it make if we follow different routes, provided we arrive at the same destination.
—Mahatma Gandhi

Chapter Seven: A: Angel Ideas

We have been talking about listening to Spirit's prompting. I call this type of prompting Angel Ideas. Ideas come to us from the One Mind. They guide us to right action. They constitute awareness. They are the Christ consciousness coming to us. These ideas are filled with light and joy. These "angels" are always with us, protecting and directing us to express who we are. They are spiritual inspiration.

Thoughts or ideas—choose wisely.

What's the difference between Angel Ideas and "thoughts?" "Thoughts" stem from the small r reality point of view. They are culture-impacted points of view. Most thoughts result in feeling a sense of fear or lack. Angel Ideas come from One Mind. An Angel Idea may produce discomfort because it asks us to move out of ruts and habitual ways of thinking, but it never suggests lack and never comes from fear.

Here are two stories about thoughts and ideas that may help illustrate the difference, and the outcome of choosing to listen to one or the other.

Story One: The cord from my laptop charger was bent and almost broken near the connection to the computer. I knew it was. I could tell the connection from the charger to the computer was getting risky to say the least. But instead of dealing with the problem I just kept wiggling and propping up the cord to get the connection.

The thoughts went like this: I don't have time to deal with this, it is going be too difficult, I am busy visiting my family, and of course—maybe if I pretend it isn't broken it won't be, or magically it will get fixed.

One day wiggling the cord was not enough. No power to the computer, only four hours left in my battery. Yikes. I called Dell.

"Sure," they said, "We will send you a new one (free on the warranty)." Bottom line: It would only take a day or two to get to me.

Easy—but two days is a long time when your business is on the computer. In addition, I was getting ready to travel again so I didn't get the part until it caught up with me five days later. In the meantime, my whole business was on hold.

Why didn't I do this before there was an emergency? The cord would have had plenty of time to reach me before I traveled and before the old one broke. It was obvious that I would need a new cord sooner or later. Why didn't I handle the problem before it became an emergency? What stopped me? Thoughts stopped me

All along my inspiration—my inner voice—was telling me to take care of this. The idea of how and when to take care of this was right there with me. The idea or inspiration—or Angel Ideas—gave me an easy solution. But I didn't listen to inspiration or ideas. I listened to thoughts instead.

Story Two: A few weeks after we moved to our new home we stopped by the Senior Center bazaar. At the bazaar, I found a fabulous set of dishes with a place setting for four people for only $5.00. Since most of our household items were in storage, I was overjoyed.

A few days later, it dawned on me I should have bought another box of dishes since we would need a place setting for eight if we were going to have my husband's family over for dinner.

I lamented over this lack of foresight for weeks. All along my little voice, my inspiration—Angel Idea—kept telling me to stop by the Center to see if just perhaps the other set of plates was not sold. Since that seemed impossible, I ignored—once again—my voice of inspiration.

I had thoughts about how hard it would be to walk into the Center and ask the question; how impossible it would be that the dishes would still be there, and on and on.

Nevertheless, one day I was walking by the Center and my inner voice spoke up. "How can you ever write about following inspiration and ideas if you won't do it yourself? Don't be shy—go in!" I walked past the Center and then I turned and walked back, went in, and stumbled through the explanation. The woman behind the counter smiled and said, "Isn't that strange, after the sale we ended up with one box of dishes."

She was happy to get the extra money for the Center and glad to dig the dishes out of storage. I was happy that I listened to the voice of inspiration and Angel Ideas. I grinned all the way home.

Most of us listen to thoughts! We listen to thoughts that tell us what won't work, doesn't work, isn't right, blah, blah, blah. What we should be listening to is—ideas. That is what our inner voice, our inspiration is giving us—ideas. These Angel Ideas are wealth. Ideas lead us to what we want, need, or desire. Ideas inspire. Ideas bring results. Ideas are directions from God.

What voice are you listening to? Is it a thought—limited, old, a common belief? Or is it an idea—which leads you to light and life?

There is another side to listening to ideas rather than thoughts. That is the side of ideas that keeps us safe from doing what we shouldn't be doing. This one is easy: If you have to rationalize what you are doing, you are thinking and not listening to ideas. Ideas almost always demand that we summon courage, but we never have to rationalize them.

Every human being has, like Socrates, an attendant spirit; and wise are they who obey its signals. If it does not always tell us what to do, it always cautions us what not to do.
—Lydia M. Child

Messengers

Angel Ideas come to us in many forms. Sometimes they are whispers in our ears. Sometimes they come in the form of inspirations or gut instinct. Often they are revealed to us through the unique expressions of others. Movies, songs, books, overheard conversations on street corners, art, friends, and strangers often deliver the Angel Idea that we need to hear. If we are open to messengers, they will appear.

An Angel Idea appeared to me one day in the form of a taxi driver.

I lived in downtown Los Angeles at the time, and I was walking to my office building about 5:00 a.m. to teach The Shift.

Of course it was dark, but I was used to walking to work in the dark and enjoyed the quiet and solitude. To get to the building I passed numerous hotels and taxis waiting for passengers. At that time of day, the drivers were usually asleep.

I had been contemplating a conference that I had attended the day before in San Francisco. It had been an inspiring and moving conference and someone had casually mentioned to me that we were all messengers of God. I was contemplating that fact, yet also concerned that I would never be as inspirational to others as the people speaking at the conference had been. I started feeling worthless.

As I passed the row of taxis, one of the doors flew open and a man jumped out in front of me. In halting English, he literally shouted at me, "God loves you!" I am sure he saw the tears spring to my eyes as he said it once more, "God loves you!" I smiled at him; he smiled at me and got back into the taxi. I still thank him for carrying the message I needed to hear that day. For me it was an Angel Idea direct from God.

There are two mistakes one can make along the road to truth—not going all the way, and not starting.
—Buddha

Compel versus impel.

Reason often makes mistakes, but conscience never does.
—Josh Billings

He who sacrifices his conscience to ambition burns a picture to obtain the ashes.
—Chinese Proverb

Another way to determine whether thoughts or Angel Ideas are guiding us is to understand the difference between the words compel and impel.

Compel means, "to cause a person or thing to yield to pressure; force, oblige, make happen." We often use the word compel when we talk about why we do things. But to compel implies fear or lack. This thinking says that if I don't do this today I will never have what I want tomorrow. It suggests that no matter what it takes to get it, do it now. Often it is a thought that asks us to rationalize our behavior, as in "the end justifies the means." To be compelled may feel like someone is pulling and tugging at us to go a certain direction. If we are paying attention, we will notice an internal discomfort when pushed by compelling thoughts.

Impel means "to set or keep in motion or action; move, actuate, drive, mobilize." It may produce the same action as compel, but with a different motivation. Impel never suggests that there is one way and one way only. It never asks us to compromise our values. It never asks us to impose upon or harm another in search of what we want. When impelled, I feel as if someone who loves me has an arm around me, guiding me, saying, "I am with you and this will be OK."

Thoughts that impel tend to ask more of us. They are more discomforting, more involved and they push us to think and take action. Impel will move us out of our ruts of how it always has been. Compel offers an easy way out. Impel has many layers. Spiritual living is harmonious and easy, but not comfortable.

Comfortable is not the goal.

Sometimes when I really don't know what path to take, I close my eyes while holding out my hands. I imagine holding one path in each hand. My motivation is God First, moving to light, listening for Angel Ideas. When I begin to feel which path feels the most light I choose it, although it is often the more uncomfortable path because it asks me to give up my habitual thinking and move out of ruts.

I grew up in a wonderful town in Pennsylvania. I always knew I wanted to move away when I grew up. I didn't know where. In my late teens, I realized it was California. At that time, it was like moving to a foreign country. I knew nothing about California or why I would want to go. It was totally impractical. I was a young mother; my husband and I had a baby son. Part of me felt compelled to stay home, and get a job. It would have been easier, but it didn't feel right.

I kept thinking I had to go, I felt impelled. I applied to a college in Southern California—still not knowing why, but I figured this would at least give us a reason to go. I was accepted. I still remember exactly where I stood in my kitchen as I read my acceptance letter. I was flooded with joy—and trepidation—as now I would have to tell people we were leaving.

There was not a rational reason to go. I did know that I wanted my husband to pursue his dream of being a professional musician and that California was the place to do this, somehow. We did not know anyone. We did not know what we could or would do once we got there, and we had only $300 (the money we had left after selling all our possessions) and a car. However, all I could see was a lighter path. We took it.

I can look back now and see all the reasons why. We both found what we were looking for by following that guidance, even though in the end it took us on separate paths.

As we listen to Angel Ideas, our desire becomes to make faith, not vice, habitual. We do this by keeping our emotions and thoughts on Truth, by putting God First.

The popular saying, "follow the light" works for practical life. Move towards the light. Listen for guidance. Be prepared to be inspired to action by innumerable Angel Ideas. Don't be afraid, Love will be leading you and those you care about the most. Love has already provided for you. You will become aware of that provision as you follow Spirit's guidance. Remember, the Infinite Loving Mind, the One, is the only Cause and Creator. What we are doing is awakening to what already exists. Eventually you will discover that you are the light.

Tracing the line of light.

Throughout history, many people have listened to Angel Ideas and then reported back to us about the limitlessness of life. I have quoted some of them throughout this book.

These people have carried forward the line of light from one generation to the next, from culture to culture. Each has provided us with more insight into the Truth of who we are.

These torchbearers have pointed out that Truth is embedded in each one of us. Although the path we walk to uncover and live this Truth is personal, there is great strength and joy to be found in traveling and sharing with others both past and present.

Many sages have spoken of these universal Laws of Spirit. If we look deep down at the fundamentals of most religions and philosophies and even quantum physics, we find these truths run through all of them.

These men and women are part of the line of light that has carried through time the words and understanding of the One Mind. They spoke in dialects that were appropriate and accessible to the time and culture in which they lived.

In his book "Consilience: The Unity of Knowledge," Edward O. Wilson argues for the fundamental unity of knowledge and the need to search for consilience—the proof that everything in our world is organized in terms of a small number of fundamental natural laws that comprise the principles underlying every branch of learning.

As the human mind becomes aware that there is more than what it knows and believes, we have begun to step out of the jail of our beliefs and into a world of "what ifs."

Every Shift, no matter how small, opens new doors and windows into the eternal All. What we allow ourselves to know (filtered through our point of view) begins to alter what appears, as our material world takes on new form.

What is really happening is that we are finally relinquishing our belief in a material world and beginning to understand that our world is not material, but Spiritual. That understanding dissolves what appears to be material so that its true Spiritual nature becomes visible to us.

Uncovering the evidence.

We must prove this for ourselves. Taking on beliefs heard but not understood only creates another paradigm or rut. In addition, if we do not bring forward to now the pieces of ourselves that were lost in past traumas and decisions, we become a parody of what God looks like rather than a clear expression of It. If not corrected, in time we are usually worse off then we were before we started our spiritual quest.

The statement about "not pouring new wine into old bottles" speaks of this truth. When that phrase was written in the Bible (Matthew 9:17), there was no way to completely clean a bottle of wine residue. If new wine was poured into this bottle, the wine would interact with the residue—a chemical reaction would take place—and the bottle would explode.

Isn't this a perfect picture of what it's like to pour new ideas into a self that has not truly cleaned out the residue of past choices and traumas?

Just saying "God is All" will not produce good results. However, living fully the true meaning of God as All, and letting go of any limiting point of view that muddies the water, allows us to see the Truth. The result of Shifting our perception to Truth appears to us as good results in our daily life, and we experience the outward symbols of God's activity.

In Chapter Eleven, *Unkink the Hose*, we will learn more about how to collect and clean up the parts of ourselves that we have left behind.

Look for evidence to prove to yourself that there is only One Mind, which is Infinitely Loving.

Take note of the times when you put God First and chose to be conscious of the State of Grace—and then what you needed became visible. Have you ever wished that God would send you an email, fax, or letter and just for once let you know exactly what is True and what you're supposed to do about it? In a very real sense God does this in every moment! But you have to pay attention to see it.

Start an evidence and coincidence log.

An evidence and coincidence log helps us become more aware of the constant presence of God in our lives. Instead of focusing emotion and attention on what is not working, we begin to look at what is working.

I have a wonderful friend who after discovering the joy of Shifting embraced the value of an evidence log with all her heart. Every day she had astonishing proofs of God's Infinite Love for her and others.

She consistently looked for what was working in her life and focused on the good, true, beautiful, and pure. I loved to get her phone calls. She would begin by proclaiming "evidence log, evidence log," with such joy and enthusiasm that I began to see her as evidence of God in my life.

What to look for? Everything that is good, true, beautiful, and pure. Begin to note the coincidences that are so much a part of our lives. Webster's dictionary defines the word coincidence as "an accidental and remarkable occurrence of events, ideas, etc., at the same time, suggesting but lacking a causal relationship."

Our whole life is composed of coincidences—which are not really coincidences, but evidence of a Divine Intelligence. Think about it. Just to have this book in your hands involved a million different things that had to happen among hundreds of people.

How could you have orchestrated even this small event? You couldn't have. It had to be One Intelligent Mind acting out of Its unfolding and expansion, which coincided within the world as you, reading this book.

Sometimes our evidence comes in the small things that remind us that everything is an activity of God. Here is an example a friend sent me not long ago: "In December 1996, shortly after I began Shifting, I traveled to Yakima, Washington, to give a speech. Before my speech, I went into the ladies' room, and as I was getting ready, I noticed that a thread had come loose on the snap on my pants, and my pants would not fasten in the front.

"It looked terrible. I asked around in the washroom looking for a safety pin. No one had one. I went out to the exhibit area and noticed a booth with a nice lady working it, selling crafts and ornaments. I showed her the problem with my pants and asked her if she had a safety pin. She thought she might. She reached into her bag and pulled out her pincushion. There in the pincushion was a needle and thread, and the thread was the exact color of my pants. We both smiled, and I sewed my pants right there."

Sometimes coincidences take on such a striking form that we are bumped out of our day-to-day living to exclaim, "How could this have happened. What are the odds?"

The more we recognize the hand of the Infinite Loving One guiding our lives, the more we see Its guidance. Writing down coincidences not only grounds them in our mind, it gives us the proof we need on days when we find ourselves momentarily feeling faithless.

I have taken on the habit of writing down evidences and coincidences on little pieces of paper and collecting them out of my pockets every night. Let me give you a few examples. On a recent plane trip, I had four slips of paper before the plane took off. Here's one:

While waiting to board the plane I overheard a mother tell her young daughter that they would not be able to sit together because the plane was full. I started to tell them that I would switch seats with them when I realized that I didn't know where we would be sitting. Once I was seated in the plane, I was not really surprised to find that the mother's seat was next to mine, and her daughter's right behind me. It was an easy switch. I smiled to myself and thanked the invisible hand of God for proof of Its existence. It's like the wind. We see the evidence of its power but not the wind itself.

Noticing evidence is the practice of being habitually aware of the qualities of One Mind all around us in every moment. This begins to create our own inner conviction of Truth. As that inner conviction gains strength and power, no amount of disagreement from others can suggest to us that there is anything other than Omnipresent Love.

Practicing sounds like work, but it is such a joyful experience, and once you start you will not want to stop. It always produces results. Usually the results appear in ways that we could never anticipate.

Years ago, before I started writing the class called The Shift I was dealing with a major lack of funds. Nothing I did changed the picture (in fact it only made it worse) so I decided to do what I felt was important for me to do and just began to write the class. During that time of uncertainty, I started practicing looking for evidence.

One day I realized that I needed to get some food in the house and decided to walk to the farmer's market. I wasn't quite sure how I was going to pay for it. After inspecting my motives for buying food, I decided that it would be right to take some money from the ATM, even though it would bring my balance to zero, if not below.

When I withdrew the money, I was very grateful that it was immediately available to me and I was grateful for the evidence of Mind's immediate provision. Walking to the market, I decided to practice looking for evidence of Love. I had no ulterior motive, I was not hoping for anything. I just wanted to acknowledge Love's place in all of my life. Here's some of what I saw.

• I noticed Love while watching a man stoop to tie his son's shoes.

• I noticed Love in the careful planting of flowers along the buildings.

• I noticed Love when I saw a businessman stop and chat with a homeless man. I overheard the conversation as I passed by. The businessman was checking on a job interview the homeless man had the day before. He wanted to know if he was going to be all right for the day.

• I noticed Love and Mind in the beauty of the building lines against the sky. I noticed Love in the placing of the streetlights so I could cross safely.

• I noticed Love everywhere, and I was moved by gratitude for Its care for all of us.

When I got to the market, it was crowded, as usual. There were hundreds of people bustling and trying to squeeze by each other. As I inched my way down one of the aisles the crowd suddenly moved away from a center spot. Everyone had his or her back to this center. I was the only one facing it. And there on the floor was a hundred-dollar bill. I picked it up and looked at this gift.

For a fleeting moment, I thought of yelling, "Did anyone drop one hundred dollars?" But I knew that the One Mind had provided it for me at that moment, as It provides for everyone in every moment. As I picked up the bill, the crowd began to mill again. I finished my shopping with an overflowing heart, filled with gratitude and a stronger conviction that Mind, Infinite Love, is always present.

The point here was not the money. The point was awareness of Love. What is needed is already provided. It is our perception of lack that keeps us in lack. Perception produces reality and what is perceived to be reality magnifies.

An interesting coincidence happened one day as I walked home after teaching The Shift. I was contemplating the power of acknowledging One Mind and hoping that I would have many examples to use for the next class.

As I walked past my apartment building, I noticed some bits of paper on the ground and picked up one in order to throw it away. It was a torn picture, and the part I was holding showed a Greek figure and a Greek column. I was still holding it when I got to my apartment.

As I walked in, I noticed a piece of paper lying on my living room couch. I assumed the wind had blown in something from outside (although this had never happened before, and has never happened since).

It was the exact duplicate of the torn piece of picture that I had picked up six floors below. In the past, I might have interpreted this coincidence from the standpoint of a mystical path. Now I understand that the only important symbol of this coincidence is that it is evidence of One Mind.

Whenever I doubt the omnipresence of God, I remind myself of the constant examples found in coincidences that make up the fabric of my life. If there is a time when it seems as if these coincidences are not as evident to me as usual, then I ask myself, am I really following God's plan—or am I being hard-headed and deaf to Angel Ideas?

When I listen to Angel Ideas and follow their guidance, it always astonishes me how much happens in a very short period of time. Recently I stopped to listen, and after yielding to direction I found that within a week's time I had a new source of income, a new home that was better than I could have even thought to ask for, a new car, and most of all, a renewed sense of yielding to the State of Grace and being witness to the outcome.

We are eternally grateful to the invisible hand who has guided us through all the obstacles of this fantastic voyage.
—Bertrand Picard and Brian Jones, after completing the first around-the-world flight in a balloon.

PRACTICAL ANGEL IDEAS.

We often miss how we have been provided for and how much we do listen to Angel Ideas because we focus so much on what isn't working. Take a moment and write what you have done in the last six months that felt light, or right, to you and what the results were. The size of the event is not important. Small things are what guide our lives. The bonus of doing this is that it puts us in the attitude of gratitude. That thankful attitude Shifts our thoughts to the unlimited abundance of Grace quickly and effectively.

In the past six months, the following wonderful events happened to me:

Its name is unknown: I simply call it Tao.
—Lao Tzu

There is only Ati [Spirit].
—Chogyam Trungpa

Space and time are not external to consciousness: Our finite system can be accounted for from the basis of an infinite system that is totally mindlike.
—Daniel A. Cowan, Mind Underlies Spacetime

Truth is one: sages call it by different names.
—The Vedas

Tao is the law of all things, of all events. Tao is the common ground of creation.
—John Heide, The Tao of Leadership

That thou art, other than whom there is no other seer, hearer, thinker or agent.
—The Upanishads

I Am that I Am: and he said, Thus shall thou say unto the children of Israel, I AM hath sent me unto you.
—Exodus 3:14, Bible

God has no religion.
—Mohandas Karamchand Gandhi

La ilaha illa 'illah. There is no god, but God.
—Mohammed

I am Brahman, the all in all.
—Aham Brahmasmi

I am the Alpha and Omega, the beginning and the ending, saith the Lord, which is, and which was, and which is to come, the Almighty.
—Revelation 1:8, Bible

Chapter Eight: C: Choose Consciously

Everything reflected in the mirror called our lives is something we have chosen. However, for the most part the choosing has been unconscious. We choose according to our upbringing and life events, our conditioned culture-impacted paradigm.

Most of the time these choices were made in a split second but have affected years of our lives. We are living lives based on decisions and choices we made when we were young, but as time passes, we continue to live lives based on those unconsciousness decisions.

Some of these early decisions did not even have a "logical" basis. Maybe we were in the kitchen and a can of soup fell on our head. At that moment, we decided we didn't like kitchens, soup, or that time of day—it could have been anything. Other choices seem to have a more "logical" reason for their existence. Perhaps we felt abandoned by someone we love, and chose never to trust in love again. Unconscious choices build and maintain small r reality.

When we are not aware of our choices, we focus on problems in our lives and think that they are problems— when actually they are symptoms.

They are symptoms of our not understanding who we really are and the source of our existence. As we continue to focus emotion on what we perceive to be real, we get more of the same.

Easier and more elegant is to focus feelings on what is True.

The message as to what is not true will either bubble to the surface like Magic 8 Balls, or the "problem" will simply wither away without our even noticing.

As we are more aware of Reality, our choices will reflect a more enlightened thought. Following the GRACIOUS steps helps to break out of ruts and paradigms. To Choose Consciously we put God First, Repent, and listen to Angel Ideas. We base our choices on the understanding that we are the reflection and expression of the Infinite Loving One. Our goal is to see and think as the One Mind sees and thinks.

Choose boldly and with commitment.

That the moment one definitely commits oneself, then Providence moves too. All sorts of things occur to help one that would never otherwise have occurred. A whole stream of events issues from the decision, raising in one's favor all manner of unforeseen incidents and meetings and material assistance, which no man could have dreamed would have come his way. I have learned a deep respect for one of Goethe's couplets: "Whatever you can do, or dream you can, begin it. Boldness has genius, power, and magic in it.

—W.H. Murray, The Scottish Himalayan Expedition

Nothing explains the results of commitment better than Goethe's statement, "Whatever you can do, or dream you can, begin it. Boldness has genius power and magic in it."

Too many of us stand with a foot on one side of an abyss and a foot on the other side and wonder why we can't move. All we're doing is hoping that the ground doesn't shake so we won't fall in.

We are paralyzed by our unwillingness to commit ourselves to an idea, whether the idea appears as a person, place, or thing.

There is a popular saying, "Be careful what you wish for, you may get it." But of course. So what? Sometimes we can't know that we don't really want something until we get it. Better to get it and find out than to be afraid of asking. Doesn't anyone ever stop and think that we could say, "Thank you, but I realize this must belong to someone else."

When I was in high school, I decided to learn how to play the guitar. I was really just trying to endear myself to my boyfriend, since he was a musician. No matter what the reason, I really, really wanted a guitar. Finally, my parents bought me a one. I practiced on it about two times and realized I just didn't want to play it. My brother did. I gave it to him and he has been happily playing it ever since. In fact, it became his life's dream to be a musician. No one lost anything by my trying the guitar. If I hadn't asked, I could still be wasting energy wanting something I really didn't want, and my brother might never have been the musician he is today.

You don't know how to make decisions? Are you afraid that if you make one you will be labeled foolish for immediately changing your mind should you decide that the first decision didn't suit you? The only foolish thing about decisions is not making them—and not changing them when we learn a better way.

A plane flying on autopilot makes about a dozen small changes in direction every minute to stay on course. That means during an hour-long flight it "corrects course" almost seven hundred and twenty times.

Amazingly, that means the entire time passengers are flying in the wrong direction, but end up in the right spot. Obviously in this case changing course is not being inconsistent. In making a decision you must commit to it, just as the plane commits to flying. You will never know what you really want unless you commit. Only then will your inner voice get your attention as to the wisdom of what you have chosen.

Decisions and logistics are two different things. Making decisions is much easier when the logistics of making it are separate from the act of deciding. Usually we put the two together. For example: moving… anywhere. The decision to move is one thing. If we add in all the logistics like how, when, where, why, what—there are too many variables to deal with. First, make the decision. Then take each logistical requirement as a decision—one at a time. Trust in your inner guidance, be ready to change direction at any moment, and decisions are no longer a stumbling block to "moving on".

When I was a child (I confess I still do this when pressed), I learned that I could easily make a decision by tossing a coin. I told myself I would abide by the coin toss, and I meant it. I would toss the coin, note the outcome, and then quiet my thought. If I found that I was disturbed by the outcome, I knew that the other path was correct for me, and I would then change my mind and go that direction.

You can accomplish the same thing by imagining that you've made a decision. Start taking concrete steps to carry it out. Give yourself a time frame—a week, a month, whatever works. At the end of that time, quiet yourself and listen. What are Angel Ideas telling you?

The answer will be clear if you are willing to listen, and willing to give up control of how you think it should be.

Be committed; trust God's rightful activity and you have stepped into Grace. Evidence and coincidence will bloom around you when you're on the right path. If you find you're not, then change your mind and take another way. Not doing so is just as foolish as continuing down the freeway after you realize that you've missed your exit. The further you travel, the more off-course you will get. Listen continually for Angel Ideas and your detours will be short.

Choose wealth over riches.

For many years I have worked with people and their money as a Certified Financial Planner, and I have I discovered that having lots of money does not necessarily mean that a person is wealthy.

The truth is, we are all wealthy and no one is poor, but that is not what the world has told us. Remember, the Earth state of mind is a game about overcoming the belief of lack. It has created a system of buying and selling, and therefore we must be "sold" on the belief that there is never enough. It really is time be aware of the game and then to know and act from the Truth of One Mind.

As we work through the GRACIOUS steps, we discover that we have always received and always will receive all that we need. As we awaken to the Truth about who we are and the truth that this is not a material, physical, mental, or mystical universe, but a Spiritual one, we will see the evidence of this in our daily lives.

Take time out to choose.

I skate to where the puck is going.
—Wayne Gretsky

Never confuse motion with action.
—Ernest Hemingway

Our days are packed with things to do. If they are
not packed, we fill them even if it is just "killing time."
When faced with mounds of things to do, we make lists
and rush off to accomplish them. We plan our days using
every second. We say that we cannot take time off for
anything not measurable.

How did this happen? How did we find ourselves
in such a state that we think we're doing something
while rushing around? The only worthwhile "doing" is
expressing who we are. It doesn't matter what vehicle we
choose to express ourselves with, but expressing ourselves
is what we must do.

Instead, we act out and express at other people. Who
have we become when we're so angry that we yell at each
other in our cars? When we don't have time to talk to
our friends and family? Who are we when we have not
chosen to take time to choose—when we do not choose
to take time to pray?

What is prayer really?

Desire is prayer.
—Mary Baker Eddy

Prayer enlarges the heart until it is capable of containing God's gift of Himself.
　—Mother Teresa

One day I was attempting to run up a hill. Since it was hard for me to do I unconsciously said something like, "God, help me up this hill." As soon as I thought it, I was stopped in my tracks by the realization that what I had done wasn't really prayer. It was a request for an improved lifestyle. An Angel idea came to me, "What does God know of your need for an improved lifestyle— God is omnipotent, omniscience and omnipresent Love, which is really Heaven here and now?"

I realized that most of the time what is called "prayer" is asking God to understand where we are, and to give us something, or change our circumstances.

I remember two very specific times when I prayed for something. They were quite important at the time. In ninth grade, I visited the church on the hill every day after school to pray that the boy I liked would like me. I was very serious about this one.

A year or two earlier, I prayed in that same church that I would be chosen as a cheerleader. I remembered promising God that I would do a better job of making other people happy if that prayer were answered.

In Bill Geist's tongue-in-cheek book Fore! Play he says, "At the Fellowship of Christian Athletes Golf Ministry booth ('impacting the world for Christ through golf'), a representative reminds us that God is all powerful and could definitely help our golf games if He or She so chooses.

"But there are famines, wars, pestilence, floods, and so forth that could distract Him or Her from lending a hand with our putting.

And we reminded ourselves that He or She just might decide to adversely affect our games, too, especially when we're playing on Sunday mornings when we're supposed to be worshiping Him or Her."

Bill may be joking—but isn't this what we all do?

What do we pray for?

We pray for all sorts of things. We pray for health for others, and ourselves, for an improved financial position (again for ourselves and others). We pray for world peace, and we pray, very unselfishly it appears, for enlightenment—so that we may be better people.

Sometimes these prayers are answered, but is it God that answers them? If they are not answered, is it God that doesn't answer them? If there is a God that can be swayed by our prayers, then this God must be like us— human in some way.

Most of us don't believe that God is made in our image and likeness—we believe we are made in God's image and likeness. Depending on the words we choose to say, we believe that God is a Higher Power, One Mind—Spiritual. Yet, we continue to pray for "human" things to change. We are attempting to use God to make our lives better.

When I use God, as the catch-all for asking for things because I think this is what "He" wants me to do, I cannot possibly understand God. What I am doing is saying, "I want a better life for myself or others." Even asking for enlightenment is a request for relief from a limited life.

On the hill that day I realized that real prayer is when we are willing.

Willing to let go, willing to do, willing to listen, willing to stop, willing to go, willing to yield. Prayer is not asking, it is not demanding, it is not will-power, it is not a request, and it is not visualizing how we want it to be. It is a willingness to "let go" and let Grace, and truly mean it when we say, "Not my will, but Thine be done." Prayer brings our awareness and perception to God, not God to us.

It is this Shift in our point of view that brings us into alignment with Truth. Once there, we can see what is already, and always will be, available to us on whatever scale we are currently able to perceive. This Shift provides the permanent "answer to our prayers." Not because our lifestyle needs to improve, but because this is the Truth of Being—the unlimited Love of Grace.

The next time I ran up the hill I prayed again, only this time it was different. My prayer sounded something like this: "I am grateful to know that I am not what appears to be a human trying to run up a hill, but in Truth I am a Spiritual being expressing the qualities that are God in every moment. The specific qualities I am grateful to be expressing at this moment are strength, grace, persistence, consistency, joy, ease..." You get the idea. The result—my perception about who and what I was doing—Shifted, so that what looked like a run up a hill became something much more joyous and in a larger sense was much more meaningful.

Prayer sets us in line with God. It does not set God in line with us. It tunes us up to receive Angel Ideas. Prayer lightens our load by enabling—Repenting—directing our thought back to the One Source, yielding to Grace. Prayer brings commitment to what we are doing.

Choosing is prayer when we are choosing to see what exists as beautiful, good, pure, and true. Choosing is prayer when we choose to see what has already been given to us, and to be grateful for the evidence of Love. Choosing is prayer when we choose to express all the qualities of the Infinite Loving One.

When our choices are our prayers, our lives are filled to overflowing with blessings. Take the time to choose, take the time to notice. Take this time first, not after all the running around. The next time you have to choose between getting something done and taking the time for personal prayer, choose yourself and prayer first.

PRACTICAL CHOOSING.

I choose therefore I am.
—Amit Goswami, The Self-Aware Universe

I wanted to change the world. But I found that the only thing one can be sure of changing is oneself.
—Aldous Huxley

Let's look at a way of choosing that will allow your life to unfold easily. We set ourselves up to fail in most choices or resolutions because we don't stop and listen to the internal voice's response to the choice. We stop short of the real choices.

I don't have to remind you, do I, that it is not things that we want; we desire instead a clearer perception and understanding of God. Choosing in this way helps us see what our small-i is telling us, which enables us to focus instead on the Truth of our being.

Here's how to choose effectively. Choose something that you have desired, intended to have, or dreamed about. Since many people desire an attractive and healthy body let's walk through how this choice might look. In the Chapter The Relationship With Our Body we will take this discussion further. In the meantime, try this:

I would first state:

I choose to have a good-looking and healthy body.

Now stop and listen. Perhaps the voice says:

"Ha, well sure you may want to have this body, but you will have to exercise to get it."

So I respond:

I choose to exercise.

Listen again. Perhaps the voice says:

"You hate to exercise."

I respond:

I choose to love to exercise.

Listen again. The voice may say:

"You don't have the time to exercise."

I respond:

I choose to have the time to exercise.

The voice:

"You don't have anything to wear to exercise."

I respond:

I choose to have something to wear to exercise.

See how this works? The list can, and probably will, run on for a page or two for just one simple choice. What we are doing by choosing consciously is uncovering, without attachment and emotion, all the hidden choices and beliefs that have kept us from actually doing the thing we thought we had resolved to do. We are Shifting our perception.

Take a moment and choose something. It doesn't matter what it is, but it might be fun to try something that you have resolved to do before that never worked. Keep listening and choosing until you feel that release that tells you there is nothing else to uncover.

Now that you have chosen, you can let this part go for now. If you find that nothing happens after a time, go back and choose again. Share with someone you totally trust this dream or choice of yours, and ask that person to let you know when you voice anything that contradicts the choice. Perhaps that person can make a choice and share it with you too. You will become the protectors of each other's dreams.

Take another moment and look back over the past six months. Write in a journal about what you chose. While reviewing, did you discover that some things happened that you did not feel you chose? What were they? What did you learn from those things that you did not consciously choose?

These questions may spark another round of conscious choices. Try doing an "I Choose" page at least once a week. You can never consciously choose too often.

My prayer is to choose _____:

I Choose:

I Choose:

I Choose:

I Choose:

I Choose

In the past six months I chose:

What happened that I did not choose?

What did I learn from what happened?

Now that you have chosen, do a qualities list for each choice and have someone ask you "Which is more important to you?" so you can put these qualities in the correct order.

The combination of choosing and knowing the qualities of the choice moves your life towards your spoken and unspoken dreams. Review how to do a qualities list by re-reading the chapter, God First.

The qualities of what I am consciously choosing:

1. _____
2. _____
3. _____
4. _____
5. _____
6. _____
7. _____
8. _____

I have a choice in every moment to keep my heart open or closed, to live in love or fear. More than any other specific practice, I have found that maintaining the awareness of choice is the most important factor in keeping an open heart, for every action, every thought, every moment contains the potential for bringing us closer to either intimacy and healing or isolation and suffering.
—Dean Ornish, M.D., Love and Survival: The Scientific Basis for the Healing Power of Intimacy

There is a vitality, a life force, a quickening that is translated through you into action, and there is only one of you in all time, this expression is unique, and if you block it, it will never exist through any other medium; and be lost. The world will not have it. It is not your business to determine how good it is, nor how it compares with other expression.

It is your business to keep it yours clearly and directly, to keep the channel open. You do not even have to believe in yourself or your work. You have to keep open and aware directly to the urges that motivate you. Keep the channel open. No artist is pleased. There is no satisfaction whatever at any time. There is on a queer, divine dissatisfaction, a blessed unrest that keeps us marching and makes us more alive than the others.
—Martha Graham

Unless this thing is consistent with the highest right, I do not want it; and if it is, I can trust God's law to establish it
—The Lord Thy Confidence (pamphlet from 1912)

Chapter Nine: I: Imagine—What If

Imagination is more important than knowledge.
—Albert Einstein

Imagination is different from visualization. The word "visualization" implies that we are using our human mind to state what we want an outcome to be. This means we are visualizing within what we already know, and our human ego small-i is the one in control.

Imagination is the ability to allow an internal image to appear that is not present to the senses. Imagination takes us out of our rut or current filter and Shifts to a much broader point of view. Imagination is faith in what we cannot measure. That faith, that imagination, no matter how small, moves the mountains in our lives.

Visualization does have a wonderful place in our lives. Athletes use visualization to perfect their performances. As a dancer, I knew I should never perform until I could visualize every detail of the dance. Thus, I could take every step apart and dance it literally in my sleep. I built and designed furniture the same way. I saw where each cut would be made, where each nail would be driven. Out of that visualization, new and better ideas would emerge because I allowed imagination to be present.

In the same vein, I loved the process of choreography because it was such a perfect way of using visualization to combine music, bodies, and steps. Nevertheless, I could get greater results if I allowed imagination to take over.

At this point, steps and ideas I had never before seen or thought would materialize.

Imagination takes us out of life, and ourselves, as we know it. When Einstein rode the light beam in his imagination to discover his famous equation, he was thinking from his imagination. He might have said to himself "Imagine—what if..."

As suggested in this wonderful quote below from Alice in Wonderland, using our imagination seems to be difficult for most of us. We have decided that either what we imagine isn't practical or that it just isn't possible.

> "I can't believe THAT!" said Alice.
>
> "Can't you?" the Queen said in a pitying tone. `Try again: draw a long breath, and shut your eyes."
>
> Alice laughed. "There's no use trying," she said: "One CAN'T believe impossible things."
>
> "I daresay you haven't had much practice," said the Queen. "When I was your age, I always did it for half-an-hour a day. Why, sometimes I've believed as many as six impossible things before breakfast."
>
> —Lewis Carroll, Through the Looking Glass

Have you ever tried imagining six impossible things before breakfast? Think what a difference we would make if everyone stretched his or her imagination muscle daily. We would find answers to questions we had not yet asked. Imagination taps into the One Mind. The result of imagination is the realization that all already exists now and is perfectly and practically possible now. This happens when we are willing to yield to the One Mind.

In Stephen King's book, *Sphere,* the monster tells the humans that the most important faculty we have is the power of our imagination.

Unfortunately, we often use that power to imagine the worst. This is often called worry. Worry disguises itself as a good quality. After all, good people worry because they have a need to make sure everything and everybody is all right. Worry as emotion—and a negative one at that—expands nothing into something. Worry builds molehills into mountains. Worry accomplishes nothing except to make things worse. It keeps our point of view on the negative. Worry is a lack of faith. To walk the Spiritual path we must give up the habit of worry. Imagine: What if God were present—and nothing else. What then?

In his book *The Holy Chariot*, Rabbi David A. Cooper also talks about harnessing the power of imagination. Imagination is the source of all temptation. If we imagine "bad" it can become depression and we will forget our purpose in life. We must fight depression, which is the husk that separates us from the divine. We must use imagination to feel the joy of being connected to God no matter what the outside senses may be presenting to us. Remember they can never tell us of anything True. They only feed back to us what we perceive to be real.

We must learn to imagine the best. Instead of "It's too good to be true," we can say, "It's too bad to be true."

Imagine—With feeling.

What makes imagination for good even more powerful is the addition of a positive feeling. If we can imagine what it will feel like as we meet and do our dreams, we are more than halfway to living them.

Once a friend attempting to inspire me to exercise said, "Imagine what it would be like having the body you want, riding down the Pacific Coast Highway in a red convertible with the wind blowing in your hair." I did. I couldn't believe how much that motivated me to live more expressly out of my true self and to express and enjoy myself through all forms of exercise.

Let's stretch our imagination muscle towards the power of good. Let's imagine Love flowing toward, around, and through each one of us—a Love of infinite proportions. This Love is God's Love. This is the Love that is always directed towards each one of us without limitation or qualification. If you could imagine how that feels, how would you be living your life?

Maxwell Maltz in *Psycho-Cybernetics* tells us that our human nervous system does not know the difference between an "actual experience and an experience imagined vividly and in detail." This is a powerful statement. We can turn this information about our human nervous system into a blessing. This is the power of Shifting our point of view to the good, the beautiful, and the true. This is the power of imagination. Rather than holding to what is not working—focusing on fears of the past, present, or future—focus on what is True, and results cannot help but be bountiful. We are focusing, not fretting. We are living expanded rut-less lives.

Imagine all the people living life in peace. You may say I'm a dreamer, but I'm not the only one. I hope someday you'll join us, and the world will be as one.
—John Lennon

Log off the program of space and time.

Often the biggest hurdle we face is that we believe it takes time to change. Let's return for the moment to the symbol (not Reality) of energy and use quantum physics again to make a point. The wave-to-particle phenomenon happens outside of time.

All that occupies time and space is our mental images and our collective agreement that there is a past, present, and future. Omnipresent, omniscient Mind transcends time and space. When we are conscious of the One Mind, time ceases to exist.

There is no time or space that determines when we will be aware of the Infinite Loving One. Time and space exist only as thought. Depending on our belief about how long things take, that's exactly how long things take. As we become more aware of our immediate-never-separated connection to the One Mind, and express it fully, we will not be tempted to log on to the virtual reality computer of time and space.

When Jesus provided loaves and fishes for the masses, not only did he show that supply is unlimited no matter what the five senses are saying, he proved that it is immediate.

In the absolute realm of Mind, there was no need to go fishing, plant wheat, and wait for it to grow, harvest it, and then turn it into bread. This will be true for us too in varying degrees depending on our current consciousness of the ever- presence of God and on the purity of our motives.

Perceive what is already here.

I want to know God's thoughts.
—Albert Einstein

If you say that you need something, you have stated that you don't have it. You have declared yourself separate from the Source. Not only does this make a sense of lack and separate existence seem real, but also makes the assumption that our personal ego is huge. We have been taught to be humble—but separating ourselves from God is not humility, it is hubris. Aligning ourselves to the only Power that exists requires a surrender of the small-i ego to the one Ego. This is true humility.

PRACTICAL IMAGINATION.

I have learned to use the word "impossible" with the greatest caution.
—Werner von Braun

Every day for the next week take five minutes and imagine…anything. Let your mind run free. At the end of the week pick five of your favorite imaginings and list what would be different for you if each were true.

Here is a report from someone who tried this exercise:

"At various times during The Shift, we have been asked to write down impossible things, at least one a day. So periodically, I will write down something I truly think is impossible. I always write the date, too.

In reviewing my personal diary periodically, I will go through my list of impossible things. I have been amazed at how many things have happened. Actually out of the eighteen things on my list, seven happened and five things took care of themselves in a different way than expected. So, twelve out of eighteen items isn't bad. Nothing is impossible."

Today I imagine:

If this were true, what would be different in my world?

Our imagination is the only limit to what we can hope to have in the future.
—Charles F. Kettering

What we need is imagination. We have to find a new view of the world.
—Richard P. Feynman

A human always acts and feels and performs in accordance with what he imagines to be true about himself and his environment.
—Maxwell Maltz

Chapter Ten: O: Obsessive Vigilance

Shifting is easy. We are continually doing it. Shifting out of ruts and low gear is harder. Habit is aggressive. It doesn't wait around to fill a void; it pushes at us continually to reestablish itself. Have you ever noticed in your life a time when you Shifted to stop doing something and found yourself days, months, or years later doing the very thing you thought you had stopped?

I had established a pattern of working out every morning. I did a different kind of workout each day to keep myself from being bored, and I had been doing this for about a year and half.

One Friday morning I got up to go work out and it dawned on me that I had not worked out all week. It was not because I thought about it and had decided to not work out. I had simply totally forgotten and had gone back into my old pattern of being at work extra early. Shifting to Grace requires eternal vigilance.

Establishing a new habit that more accurately reflects our true nature does not happen by asking ourselves if we want to do it. People often wonder how I get up so early. They think I ask myself each morning, "Do you want to get out of bed" and I answer, "Yes."

The trick is, I never ask my small-i what it wants. That self—Beca—the material self that thinks it is who I am, would probably never want to get out of bed in the morning. Beca definitely wants to stay in bed longer.

Beca wants to stay in all the ruts she has so comfortably established for herself. However, I let my inner true Spiritual self guide me, which means I get up early most of the time.

Every man is where he is and what he is because of his established habits of thoughts and deeds.
—Napoleon Hill

Old habits die hard.

Here are two great stories about habits. You probably know the old story of the square roast. A husband was watching his wife cut off the ends of the roast before she put it in a pan. He asked her why she was doing this.

She responded that she did it because her mother did it. "Why" he asked. She didn't know so she asked her mother. Her mother responded, "Because my mother did it." Finally, they asked her mother. "Oh," she replied, "I had to do that to fit it into the pan."

Another great example is the story of why railroad tracks are 4 feet 5.8 inches wide.

Here's the order of how it happened. The people that designed and built the first railroads in America were brought over from Europe. In Europe the width of the railroads is 4 feet 5.8 inches wide. It's simple; they reproduced what they had done before. Just as we all are prone to do.

But, why were the rails that exact distance apart in the first place? Answer: Wagon wheels were that distance apart. When the train rails were built, they reproduced what they knew.

Why were wagon wheels always just that distance apart? Answer: If any designer tried to design outside of that width, they ran the risk of wheels not running in the ruts already created by other wagon wheels.

Why were wagon wheels designed that far apart in the first place? Answer: Roman chariots had already caused ruts in the road. When designing updated versions of the chariots—wagons—it was considered easier to go with the width set by the chariots.

Finally, why were Roman chariot wheels that far apart? Answer: We have finally reached the real reason for the choice of 4 feet 5.8 inches. In Roman times, it was an obvious and perfectly practical reason. Two horses pulled the Roman wagons. In order to balance out the chariot perfectly the wheels had to be this strange width to accommodate two horses' rear ends. And now—over 2,000 years later—we are still riding on rails that are based on the width of two horses' rear ends!

How many things are we doing because that's how it's always been? Moment by moment we need to question why we are doing what we are doing. Imagine outside of how it has always been. Live from an infinite Truth and life expands.

Types of habits.

Once you realize that the world is your own projection, you will be free of it, a guru told his followers, everything existing around you is painted on the screen of your consciousness. The picture you see may be ugly or beautiful, but in either case you are not bound by it. Rest assured, there is no one who has forced it on you.

You are trapped only because of your habit of mistaking the imaginary for the real.
—Aldous Huxley

There are many types of habits. A very popular one is the habit of struggle, which often turns up in another of its forms, the habit of poverty. I realized recently how intrusive the habit of struggle was for me. Although I was no longer always cash poor, I wondered why life had not expanded more fully for me in the area of money.

I didn't attach emotion to this question, but continued to express, as clearly as I knew how, my Spiritual identity as a idea of the Infinite Loving One. While walking down the street one day I had an Angel Idea news flash. "You have a habit of struggle. You have never stepped out of it because you are so good at it."

I am good at it. While raising my three children and being the wife of struggling musicians I learned how to live well within limitations. I made my own furniture and clothes, I bargain shopped, worked extra jobs, painted, pasted, hooked rugs, and traded services so that I looked like I had more cash than I did.

Someone once said to me, "I wish I had the money you do." If that person had known that I had less than $10 in the bank, I'm sure he would have withdrawn his wish. I learned to enjoy the creativity of making struggle not look like a struggle.

However, I forgot to translate the enjoyment of creativity into a bigger picture that no longer involved struggle but was simply the expression of infinite supply.

Wake up.

Who are you? I am awake.
—Buddha

Are we awake? If we're awake we're moving into the state of Grace and waking out of the hypnotic state of the conditioned worldview. When I was in my first year of college, my philosophy class teacher gave us the Four Steps of Hypnotism. If we analyze these, we can see how we have agreed to participate in our own hypnotism, or how we succumb to the master hypnotists, our culture, and the worldview.

It is no exaggeration to say that every human being is hypnotized to some extent, either by ideas he has uncritically accepted from others, or by ideas he has repeated to himself or convinced himself are true.
—Maxwell Maltz

1. Agree to play by their rules.

This first step is so important. We agree to participate in someone else's stated rules. This is consent. Consent in any culture constitutes contagion. We know it as the power of suggestion.

In October of 1998, Oprah staged a demonstration on her show. She told her audience as they were waiting for the show to begin, they were going to release a strong odor. They were told this over and over again. Although they never did release an odor, some of the audience members gave detailed descriptions of what it smelled like.

We agree constantly to the rules that our families, friends, and the world have made. What makes them true? Nothing at all, except our agreement. We have agreed to play by "their" rules in order to fit in and survive.

2. Agree to something that you know is not true.

The stereotypical hypnotist tells patients that they are sleepy. They agree even if it is not true. How many times on a daily basis do we agree to something we know is not true? For example: An overwhelming number of us have agreed that there is not enough—of anything. We believe and accept the worldview of lack. We don't have enough time, money, love, patience, joy, peace, food, pleasure, understanding…Yes? And yet in the core of our being we know this is not true.

Even if we have had only the briefest glimpse of God's State of Grace, we know that there is an infinite amount of everything. In every glimpse of God, we gain a deeper conviction that the Infinite Loving One is All, and as Its reflection we have all that It is.

3. Turn your thought inward.

This is a surprising part of hypnotism, but on closer analysis, the truth of it appears. What the hypnotist is asking us to do is close our eyes and become alone. When we pull back and turn inward to where we no longer feel the connection to others, we have separated ourselves from Divine Love. In this state of mind, we isolate ourselves, thinking no one would understand.

We hide in our homes and our bodies so that we will not have to participate or come out and play. When things start getting worse, instead of seeking help outside ourselves we retreat, hoping no one will notice. Actually, we believe that no one is noticing and that's why we retreat. Like babies who think they are hidden when they cover their eyes, we think that when we can't see out, no one can see in.

This state of mind keeps us from seeking both physical and spiritual assistance. Hypnotic suggestion gains power when we are isolated.

4. Agree not to do something that you know you can do.

Finally our hypnotist says something like, "You can't raise your arm." We agree even though we know we can raise it. Think back. What did you love to do as a child that you thought you were pretty good at? Did anyone ever tell you either that you couldn't do it or that it just wasn't done the way you wanted to do it, and you agreed?

When I started college, I thought about being an architect. A counselor actually took me around the college and showed me the rooms where the architects were studying, so that I could see that they were all men. He also reminded me that my weakness was math, and of course, I would need a lot of that. Without a fight, I backed off and switched to interior design. This turned out not to be what I wanted and I continued to switch majors for a while, looking for what felt right. It might have been architecture if someone had encouraged me, or if I had not already agreed that I could not do it.

Let's wake up to Truth. To correct a habit or move into Truth does not involve more hypnotism. Using hypnotism to cure something is like altering a shadow. It is trying to solve what appears as a physical problem with another even deeper physical problem. Let's add more light to whatever appears as a problem. We are waking out of our darkness and moving into light, not fixing a symptom.

Break the spell.

Facts do not cease to exist because they are ignored.
—Aldous Huxley

To break a spell, whether cast intentionally or unintentionally, we must first recognize that it is not a spell at all. It is only a suggestion, an illusion. It has no power but the power we give it by believing in its reality. Remember, since there is only One power—God—then there is no reason to fear another power that actually does not exist.

If someone says we can't do something, we don't have to agree. We start first with who we truly are—each of us is the expression of Divine Mind. We listen to the Angel Ideas' guidance as to our motivation. We declare what we know to be True, and the spell is broken.

Sometimes the hardest thing to do is to continue stating and believing that we do know even when it feels like we don't. Repeating to ourselves "I don't know" puts us into the hypnotic mental state of not knowing.

Wake up. State that you do know. Don't continue to fall into the loop of untrue suggestions. In the core of yourself, you know. There is no other Truth.

Since we are the Am in I Am, we do know. When the spell is broken, we will remember.

Do not believe what your teacher tells you merely out of respect for the teacher.
—Buddha

Virus protection for our minds.

Evil (ignorance) is like a shadow—it has no real substance of its own, it is simply a lack of light. You cannot cause a shadow to disappear by trying to fight it, stamp on it, by railing against it, or any other form of emotional or physical resistance. In order to cause a shadow to disappear, you must shine light on it.
—Shakti Gawain, Creative Visualization

As part of my personal commitment to provide perception-Shifting information to as many people as possible I put a lot of information out on the Internet. As a result, my email is in many people's mailboxes. Every time a new computer virus comes out, I am flooded with emails containing the virus.

I have a few choices. First, I could stop participating in the Internet. This choice I can't make because I wish to remain in integrity with God, and because I know one of the rules of the Earth game is to participate and express who we are. My second choice is to protect myself from the viruses. This is the choice I make. I protect myself by being aware of the danger and by always having and using the latest virus protections.

This is a perfect example of the necessity of Being Aware of the difference between signs and symbols of what is True and the reversal of what is True. Jesus told us to be as wise as serpents and as harmless as doves.

Just because we know the untruth and powerlessness of evil does not mean it is smart to ignore it or pretend that it doesn't claim to exist. In this case, it exists because there are those, who not knowing their God-self, are being used as tools for evil to claim its presence. The Internet as a symbol of our Oneness is also a symbol of what can happen when we allow human will and greed to take over.

When human will is in control it is much easier for evil to use us to make itself appear real. Yes, there are some people who seem to love being evil's pawn. Trying to understand why isn't going to help either them or us. As we acknowledge the Truth, we will know how to combat the virus and also free them from evil's hold.

One way that evil maintains a hold on all of us is by using the quality of curiosity to get our attention. Curiosity in itself is a wonderful thing. In the hands of someone who is manipulating our curiosity to get us to participate in evil, it is not.

For example, when the computer viruses arrive by email, the virus protection program asks me what I want to do with it. I can delete it, contain it, or try to "cure" it. Until I knew better I would be tempted not to delete it—just in case I wanted to know what it was. Then, even after it was deleted, the email carrying it would still be in my in-box and I would have to suppress my curiosity to open it before I completely trashed it.

If we remember that the worldview—the conditioned mind, our personality and glittering image—does not want us to know God because that knowledge will destroy it, we will be less tempted to participate in any of evil's attempts to be pleasurable.

How many times do we have to be told?

Success is never final.
—Winston Churchill

As in many activities, dance is something that is practiced over and over again. The ballet barre is a perfect example of using repetition to achieve perfection. No matter where in the world a ballet class is being taught, it is taught basically in the same way. As a beginning ballet student, everyone learns the same steps that the most advanced performer is still doing many years later, every day.

Standing at the ballet barre, the students hear the same instructions, over and over. Pull up, straighten your knees, and bend from the hip, stretch out—over and over and over again, from beginner to advanced.

There is a purpose to saying the same thing over and over again. It is to assist the students in building a strong base that will allow them to "fly" later. It is to help learn what is important and what is not necessary.

Beginner dancers use every part of their body to do even a small movement, and that is why a beginner often appears awkward. The polished dancer uses only what is necessary. The grace of dancers shines through in what they are not doing as much as in what they are doing. Doing it over and over again you learn to let go of what is not necessary to achieve the movement. It is learning to balance strength and stretch in order to achieve what looks like effortless movement.

One time I had a revelation while taking a ballet class. After ten years of taking class, the teacher said the same thing she always said, and I heard it differently.

In fact, I heard it so differently that a light bulb went on in my head that totally changed how I approached dance from that day forward.

Why? Because we change our perceptions in every moment, depending on a large variety of circumstances. And it is our perceptions that determine what and how we see and hear and act. I had finally advanced enough, or cleared enough other stuff out, to hear it so differently that I shifted to a completely new level of perception.

It is not a bad thing that we are told over and over and over. It is a good thing. Each telling Shifts us, and each time we act on what we learn Shifts us again and then the next telling brings us higher—in an ever-expanding circle. This is not a circle that brings us back to where we started from, but an expanding spiral that brings us around to hear it again, in a new way.

How many times do we have to be told anything? We have to be told over and over. All lessons are basically the same. Instead of despairing over this, we should rejoice. Someone loves us enough to keep reminding us of our innate perfection. We keep Shifting our perceptions and growing enough to hear it differently. There is no greater feeling than hearing the same thing we have always heard and hearing it so differently that the world Shifts into brighter hues.

No matter what your dream is, it involves the same lessons as a ballet barre. Using what is necessary in each moment and letting go of what is not achieves grace in all areas of life. Going back to how it was…is not going forward. Repetition can sometimes be a beautiful thing. It lifts us up and out to greater heights of awareness. Keep telling and keep listening. Revelation is a shift of perception to what has always been here.

Habit with him was all the test of truth, it must be right: I've done it from my youth.
—George Crabbe

Breakdown to breakthrough.

Sometimes we learn the hard way. Sometimes we break down. The choice is ours as to what to do with this opportunity. If we choose to add more negativity to what already feels negative we have entered the "dense zone."

We have chosen to play the duality game. We have attached emotion to the negative. We ask, "Why would God do this to us?" We have made God a creator of "bad." We are thinking that there is both good and bad. We are reverting to the habit of separation.

The only way to overcome this separation is to continually acknowledge that God is present wherever we are, and to recognize that in Reality everything is an activity of God.

If we choose to see the untruth of the breakdown, and use it to reaffirm who and what we are, we enter the "zone of light." With this Shift in perception, the resulting breakthrough will bless us and those we love. We will have become more like the Truth of our being, the expression of Infinite Love. We will inspire and encourage.

Shift what you perceive to be reality. Ask yourself, "What does this situation suggest I believe to be reality?" Then return to placing God First and acknowledging Spiritual Reality.

Seek and ask.

Knowing that God supplies us in every moment with everything we could ever hope for does not relieve us from the responsibility to express ourselves and take action. As we Shift out of our ruts and hear Angel Ideas, we get glimpses of ideas about things to do. These are usually not big things to do, like Joan of Arc's gathering of an army, but smaller, more day-to-day actions.

Such an action may not even seem related to anything we are working to accomplish. It could be as simple as taking a walk to the corner, calling a person, writing a letter, or smiling at a stranger. Although following these Angel Ideas may not always appear to us to have direct results, we can be sure that it does have results. Sometimes we can look and see how taking just one seemingly small step changed the course of our lives.

Take what action?

If you don't have the full approval of your conscience and your reason, you'd better not do the thing you're contemplating.
—Napoleon Hill, Think and Grow Rich

How do we know which thoughts to follow, after all Maxwell Maltz said we have 50,000 negative thoughts a day. We can all tell stories of following a thought that was not the wisest course of action. In the Chapter entitled Angel Ideas, we talked about the difference between impel and compel, and thoughts and ideas. There is another way we can be Obsessively Vigilant about our actions to more carefully ensure that we are following wisdom.

There are three steps to taking action. As with a three-legged stool, all three steps are necessary for a firm foundation.

• The first step is, allow an idea to appear. These Angel Ideas are true wealth and are always present; we just need to be willing to recognize them.

• The second step is, wait for a positive feeling about the idea. If you have an idea to make soap and nothing moves you from within about this idea, pass on it or pass it on.

• The third step is to know the mission of the idea, i.e., the way to do it. If you have an idea to make soap and you feel wonderful about it, the next step is to find out how to make soap. We don't need to know everything about soap making, just enough to get started. Perhaps it is a trip to the library, or calling a friend.

Wait patiently for each step in the triangle of action and then do it!

The heights by great men reached and kept / Were not attained by sudden flight, / But they, while their companions slept, / Were toiling upward in the night.
—Henry Wadsworth Longfellow

See miracles.

Universal Law is impartial and unemotional.
—Stewart Wilde, Miracles

Sometimes we wait for what we call miracles. Not only is this waiting not a form of action, we are waiting for something that is already always happening. All there is are miracles. That's right, only miracles.

When our perception is in tune with the song of the Infinite Loving One, we are privileged to see more and more proofs in our life that there is only One Mind.

A miracle in the traditional sense cannot be true. This is the miracle that steps in and changes a situation in such a wonderful way that it must be miraculous. It implies that the Laws of God can be broken or sidestepped. This kind of miracle has us praying to a god that arbitrarily grants favors to those he thinks have prayed the wisest and need him the most. This is not Infinite Love in action. This is the result of shifting a personal paradigm that believes that God brings both good and evil and can be charmed into changing and bending his rules for us. This shifted paradigm can often produce the result we are asking for, and we call it a miracle. If health issues are involved, we call it a faith healing.

This is not the providence of One Mind. This One Mind knows nothing about the stories we tell of the illusions we live. Infinite Love just exists. As we shift our paradigms to include this understanding, and begin to take informed action in thought and deed, our world does Shift and produce what others call miracles. In this case these are not miracles, but Reality.

We heal any situation by knowing the eternal perfection of the One Mind. We know that as we align our thought with our highest understanding of what God sees and thinks we will live miraculous lives. Thus the statement "It is too good to be true," is backwards. The statement should read, "If it is good, it must be True." The river of abundance is always flowing. We just have to step in! Miracles are God's Laws in operation, in every moment.

Stay in Truth.

Never let present results dictate the image of what you hold in your mind.
—Florence Shinn

As we begin the Shift from rut living to unlimited abundance we will begin to notice people, places and things that are having a problem. As part of that noticing, we may begin to feel that we need to "fix the problem."

If fixing the problem requires us to go down to the problem, we must not make that choice. The wisest way to fix a problem is to apply what we know of Truth to it. If we can begin to see whatever looks like a problem as a reversal of Truth, or a hidden symbol of Truth, the problem will either dissolve or correct.

There is a wonderful story in the Bible in the book of Nehemiah about not "coming down." If we take the rebuilding of Jerusalem's walls as symbolic in the One Mind's language, we can see what the storyteller was trying to tell us.

The storyteller explains how the walls (defenses) of the city (thought) were destroyed by the enemy. Has this ever happened to you? It is a time of great vulnerability. The King's cupbearer (the part of you that is strong and protective of you) goes to the King (the part of you that knows who you are) and asks permission to rebuild. Of course, permission is granted. Nehemiah travels to Jerusalem and gathers others to begin the building. Not long thereafter, a messenger from the enemy, Sanballat, arrives with an invitation. "So hey—let's get together and talk" (let's do lunch).

Now why would the person who has destroyed our city suddenly be interested in talking? Because we are taking our life back, rebuilding our protection. He knows that he had better get to us before the walls are up. Some of us, thinking that it would only be right and kind (to whom?), go down and meet with the enemy.

I cannot begin to count the times I have "gone down" to meet with the enemy. What happened? My walls were broken down once more and I had to begin the repair process all over again. One day, I realized who I must be kind to first. Guess!

Moreover, you must be kind to yourself first, too! Do not go down! In this wonderful story, Nehemiah uses some of his manpower to build and some to protect what they had built so far. Finally, Nehemiah sent his own messenger saying, "I am doing a great work, so that I cannot come down…" (Nehemiah 6:3)

Truth does not go down, it brings up. Those who do not want to let go of limited personal beliefs are often unhappy when we chose to move "up" to Truth. In the seventies, everyone around me was drinking and using some form of recreational drug. Although I wanted to be part of the group, I immediately knew that it was the wrong decision for me. That didn't stop others from trying to talk me into participating. The favorite argument—knowing of my desire to be of service—was, "How will you know how to help others if you haven't experienced their lifestyle?" Carried to its logical conclusion this is absurd since it would mean everyone should live in utter depression and poverty before they are of value to the world. Yet most of us have accepted a version of this argument at one time or another. Do not go down.

However, it is important to take the information that we're learning and apply it to our lives in practical ways. It does not do any good to sit around and think about how wonderful God is while our children are hungry. We are expected to take action while knowing Truth.

I was reminded of this one time when doing laundry. I had methodically piled the coins on my kitchen counter, pulled the laundry together and headed down the hall of my apartment building. It was only after I arrived at the laundry room that I realized I had left the quarters on the counter. Without the money, all my careful preparation was useless.

In the same way, all the studying and understanding in the world will be of no use if we leave it on the counter. We need to take what we know and put it to use. One day we will witness with full clarity that we do not have to die in order to reach Heaven, we are already in it.

In the meantime, utilize what you know now to begin to heal the world within you, the world close to you, and the world that appears far from you. Know the Truth, and it will set you and all of us free. To heal the world, remember you are the world, because what is "outside" is actually "inside." Start here.

Knowledge is of no value unless you put it into practice.
—Huber J. Grath

Redefine yourself.

The only lasting way to improve the quality of our lives is to improve the quality of our perceptions. The highest perception is to know the Truth about who we all are, and to always base our actions on that Truth.

We will begin to build our own internal knowing that cannot be shaken as we collect evidence and express gratitude for what we have been given. If we are diligent in this process, we can live lives of continuous gratitude in the State of Grace.

PRACTICAL OBSESSIVE VIGILANCE.

One of the greatest gifts we have received is the gift of camaraderie. We can use this gift to our advantage if we join together within small mastermind groups and choose to live the principles of God as we build our lives.

"Mastermind Alliance" is a term Dale Carnegie coined to describe the power unleashed when two or more people are working together in harmony toward a common goal. The goal should be a shared sense of mission.

Pick those whose purpose you believe in and understand and who believe in and understand yours. It is a given that their integrity level must be at least on the same level as yours.

With this group of people that you trust completely, begin meeting to share your dreams and the actions that you are taking to complete them.

Pay attention to habits by using this personal journal and questionnaire:

I noticed the following daily habits.

This is the habit I would like to change.

This is how I would feel if I changed this habit.

The smallest fact is a window through which the infinite may be seen.
—Aldous Huxley

Chapter Eleven: U: Unkink The Hose

When a train goes through a tunnel and it gets dark, you don't throw away the ticket and jump off. You sit still and trust the engineer.
—Corrie Ten Boom

Our faith comes in moments. Our vice is habitual. Yet, there is a depth in these brief moments which constrains us to ascribe to them more reality than all other experiences.
—Ralph Waldo Emerson

At this point we have done all the right things. We have put God First, Repented, tuned in to listen for Angel Ideas, Chosen Consciously, Imagined what we wish to see, practiced Obsessive Vigilance and still nothing changes. In fact, it may feel as if things have gotten worse. What is happening?

Have you ever attached a hose to the water faucet, turned on the water and nothing came out? Baffled, you look back at the hose and notice a kink that is blocking the flow of water. This is a perfect picture of what has happened.

We don't need to hook ourselves up to our supply. We have always been hooked up to the Source called One Infinite Mind. We don't need to turn on this Source, since it is always "running." Having understood this, we have stepped out into life with our hose—and still only a drop of water comes out.

This is not a result of God's law not working; it is because we have not shifted our perception to include the presence of God. There is a kink. In this case, the hose gets kinked when we believe, or act out of the belief, that there is more than one power and/or that we are separate from the One Power. This kink takes many forms and blocks our view of Heaven.

> *Ye shall know the truth and the truth shall set you free.*
> —Jesus Christ

The world is the mirror.

To discover the kinks in the abundance hose, it is helpful to know what to look for. Often we are so involved with day-to-day living that we do not really know what our belief system is. An easy way to discover it is to look at the life we are living and then ask: "What does this tell me about what I think is true?"

In this instance, we are using the 2nd and 3rd Steps to Shift. We are Becoming Aware and Understanding Signs and Symbols. The world acts as a mirror. Since everything begins with our point of view, then what we see outside ourselves is what we first believed to be true internally.

We can interpret what our world mirror reflects back to us in two ways. We can ask if it is a symbol of what is True or the opposite of what is True.

If it is a symbol, then you can ask yourself what qualities of God does it represent. Then use this symbol as a guide to help you understand and be grateful for what already exists and is yours now in the highest form you perceive through your current understanding of Reality.

If it is the opposite of what is True, you can easily turn back to the First Law—God First. This will counteract any claim that it may be making as to what is really True.

Turning to God First works for two reasons. First: As we Shift our perception to Truth, that Shift must yield results—as all perception governs reality. Second: As we become conscious of the Truth, our human mind yields to the Spiritual One Mind, which is always present. We have entered the realm of Grace. Then what once appeared as a material world Shifts to appear to us more as it really is, Spiritual.

Let's look at a simple example of these two ways to see a symbol. In the fall we see animals busy preparing for winter. As symbols, they are representing the qualities of diligence, caring, support, and love for themselves and their families.

On the other hand, you may see these very same animals getting into things and causing trouble as they prepare for winter. This would be the opposite of what was True. To correct the problem, go Back to One and see the qualities as they really are.

Both involve flexing your spiritual muscle and thought process. As you do this, you continue to build your inner conviction of Truth.

Temptations

Question whether your automatic thoughts are actually yours.
—Alan Loy McGinns, The Power of Optimism

What all kinks do is block our view of what is real and eternal and the abundance that is already present. All kinks in the hose have their basis in temptation.

When Jesus was tempted by the devil, he did not accept the temptation as coming from within. Even though the devil spoke in Jesus' voice, Jesus was clear that it was an untrue suggestion and not part of him. His statement "Get thee behind me Satan" explains perfectly what we are to do when faced with temptations.

Before we look at what these temptations are, let's be clear that a temptation is not a statement of fact, but a request to us that we believe a suggestion. Actually, request is much too polite. This suggestion often comes to us subtly, but it is actually a demand upon us to believe a falsity parading as Truth.

Here are some temptations that the voice (claiming to be our own) says to us and wants us to believe. The first temptation revolves around the suggestion that the Principles that we have been learning about don't really work. This is a temptation not to believe that there is an Infinite God, One Mind.

The second temptation declares, "OK so what. Even if there is a God, It isn't here for me." This temptation separates us from God and everyone else. It appears to make our case special.

The third temptation says, "Yes, God's principles work, but not all the time." This statement does not carry one element of truth, since Principle or Law based on Truth always works. It is impossible for it not to work, since God is All-Powerful.

The next set of temptations moves us into different types of ruts. There is the suggestion that it is good to suffer. To some of us this is a treasured statement. We have suffered so much that we hope there's a good reason. But God, perfect Love, could not have made us to suffer.

Our suffering is a result only of being out of tune with Reality. One result of suffering is that it can hasten us to God First and to tune into and receive the blessings that naturally follow from being one with the One Mind. Staying in suffering is not required, necessary, or desirable. Suffering is sin. It is missing the mark. As in all cases of missing the mark—we will suffer only as long as we believe that it is right to suffer.

The temptation to be a victim is similar. We can get quite a bang for our buck with this one in the material world, as we can bend others to our will by claiming to be and acting from a state of victim-hood. However, putting God First and Repenting will immediately eliminate any desire to remain a victim.

And then there is the subtlest temptation of all. It is the temptation to believe that there is comfort in matter. As we become more and more in tune with what is True, as we understand how to change things back into thoughts, and thus live from Infinite Love, our material circumstances begin to change for the better, and this is good. However, as this occurs we are tempted to become comfortable with the results. We are tempted to think that all we were doing was attempting to better our material circumstances. We are tempted to forget that our goal is to wake up to Truth, not to be comfortable in what is not true.

Fear

Only the fearless are free.
—Guy Finley

A huge view-blocker is fear. Fear is the result of doubt. A basic fear surfaces when we are tempted (more temptation!) to believe that we are not connected to God or that God is not the Only Power. This fear suggests to us that there is no solution to our problem, whatever it is. Or we are afraid that if help ever comes, it will be too late. Sometimes the fear is just that the negative, nagging voice in our head really is our own voice. None of these suggestions are true, because we are never separated from God.

A Sunday school teacher asked her class if they thought they would be afraid if they were in the middle of the ocean all alone. The entire class affirmed that yes they would be, all except one little boy. When asked why he wouldn't be afraid he said, "God would be with me."

"How do you know that God would be with you?" she asked.

"Because I would be there," he replied.

When it is dark enough, you can see the stars.
—Ralph Waldo Emerson

Addiction

Those who are unhappy have no need for anything in this world but people capable of giving them attention.
—Simone Weil

Addictions of any kind block our view and kink our hose. Addiction keeps us feeling separate. We are all aware of the "big" addictions like drugs and alcohol. However, there is an addiction that all of us fall prey to if we are not watching our thought carefully; it is an addiction to the life we live.

We may not like our life, but we know how it works. We are afraid that if we let go and Shift, things will change, which of course they will. However, for many of us, change means that since we will not know what is coming next, we will not be able to control it. Addiction of all kinds has one cure at its core. It is becoming aware of being connected and cared for by the One Love. Then we can let go and yield as the first Spiritual Law demands of us.

The willing contemplation of vice is vice.
—Arabic proverb

Abuse

People who are willing to give up freedom for the sake of short-term security, deserve neither freedom nor security.
—Benjamin Franklin

Abuse blocks our view whether we are on the receiving or the giving end of it. Sometimes the greatest abuse is occurring within our self to our self. Unless we are observant, we might miss it.

During the time that I was experiencing a drought of cash flow, I had to drop off a document in Beverly Hills. I had exactly one dime and one quarter in my pocket, and parking in Beverly Hills is very expensive. I managed to find an out-of-the-way parking slot. I pulled out my quarter and popped it in, figuring it would be just the time I needed to drop off the document. Then I read what the meter said. I realized that I could have just put in my dime. On this day, I had been practicing listening to the internal "monkey mind" and at that point it went crazy.

The tirade went on for quite a while, but what it said in essence was "How could you be such a complete idiot? Even an idiot knows how to spend money better than you do. You are such a loser and it is no wonder you don't have any money."

Wow! I could not believe the abuse over just one quarter. The only thing that the voice said that had any truth in it was "No wonder you don't have any money." How was I ever going to see the abundance that was mine when I was hosting an abusive voice that told me I was more than incompetent and that there was never enough for me?

I would never have let a person stay in my house who spoke to me that way. I would have been shocked to hear someone else say that to anyone, and would have been quick to defend the one who was attacked. "How long had this been going on," I wondered.

I began the process of kicking out the abuser because I knew it was not an Angel Idea. It was not my thought. It was not true. For me the easiest way to rid myself of internal abusive thoughts is to give the voice a form, make it a monster, a person, a dragon, whatever is appropriate for the moment. In my thought I turn and confront the abuser, tell it I will not be spoken to that way nor treated in that manner, and that it is not telling the truth. I then do something to get rid of it, even if it is just kicking it out my mental door.

The first step in ridding oneself of this insidious pest is to listen to what it has been telling us about ourselves for all of our life. The next step is to realize that this is not your voice even if it sounds like it. Of course, it sounds like you. How else could it get you to listen?

Then the next step is to do as Jesus did—command it to get behind us.

Symbolic doors.

Anything that requires us to go through a symbolic door to get to God and Infinite Love acts as a kink in the hose. This includes putting our faith in superstition, luck, ghosts, cycles, preachers, people, or channeling to the exclusion of God. It includes the belief that money or time defines the quality of our life. We kink our hose when we accept other people's thoughts as our own, refuse to forgive, or not notice that one door is closed and another is open. Our hose gets kinked when we have a conflict of values, ask for the "wrong" thing, hold on to paradigms, or host depression.

Fighting

If we could read the secret history of our enemies, we should find in each man's life sorrow and suffering enough to disarm all hostility.
—Henry Wadsworth Longfellow

At the end of the talk, someone from the audience asked the Dalai Lama, "Why didn't you fight back against the Chinese?" The Dalai Lama looked down, swung his feet just a bit, then looked back up and said with a gentle smile, "Well, war is obsolete, you know." Then, after a few moments, his face grave, he said, "Of course the mind can rationalize fighting back…but the heart, the heart would never understand. Then you would be divided in yourself, the heart and the mind, and the war would be inside you."

It is hard to consistently experience God's ever-flowing Love when we are kinking Love's supply because of conflict. Usually the conflict is within—and it is expressed outwardly to those around us. We handle conflict in three ways:

• By fighting and not listening to each other because we are too busy arguing our points.

• By avoidance, no one wants to talk about it.

• Facing it in a way that will remove the kink by validation—where we listen to each other, validate each other's point of view, and reconcile.

What will never work is fighting. When we battle the human mortal mind, or evil beliefs in any form, we give it the power it needs to exist. If we are fighting we are not aware, or conscious of, the One Love and our emotion is in fear. This is why wars create more of the same problem.

Overcoming whatever appears as evil by understanding Truth, and forgiving those who have become the pawns of evil, at times seems more than we can do. Nevertheless, we can, and we must.

We cannot ask God to help us fight our enemies, as God does not know any enemies. This is trying to use God to get what we want. Not only will it not work, but also in doing so we become the problem. Peace comes to everyone as we declare the Truth of each person and situation.

Men never do evil so completely and cheerfully as when they do it from religious conviction.
—Blaise Pascal

Are we asking amiss?

Jesus said, "Ye ask, and receive not because ye ask amiss, that ye may consume it upon your lusts." (James 4:3) If we are not getting what we want, we may be asking amiss. But what did Jesus mean? Perhaps we are asking for the thing instead of the understanding of Truth, or the quality. For example:

• We may be asking for something that is only for our material completion or pleasure. Maybe what we want is not right for us.

• We may not be acting or thinking within the Principles of unconditional Love.

• We may not have put God First.

• It may be harmful to others or ourselves.

Another reason you may not be receiving what you are asking for is maybe you are not asking big enough. Have you ever applied for a job and were turned down? Perhaps you thought, "I could have done that job easily." Maybe that was the problem. It wasn't big enough to allow you to grow more Godward.

During my cash flow drought, I finally decided to go back to a day job to supplement my writing and consulting. However, no matter what I applied for I was constantly turned down. I finally realized that I was just looking for a job to pay my bills, the easier the better. I was not looking to express Infinite Mind in any of them. I woke up to the understanding that I had to stretch myself and do what I was really qualified to do, even though at the time Beca was not too happy about it. Of course, I got that job and it blessed everyone, including me.

There are more tears shed after answered prayers than unanswered ones.
—St. Teresa of Avila

We are often protected from our choices. During the time I was looking for jobs, I applied for what appeared to be the perfect job for me, and it seemed I was the perfect person for it too. I didn't get it. Since I was positive it was the perfect job for me I couldn't understand what had happened. Years later a scandal broke around the people I would have been working for. Had I landed that job I would have walked right into the middle of it. In fact, the person who held that job ended up in jail. I was protected, even though at the time I thought I was being denied.

Think bigger than today and your tiny day-to-day needs. Pick a dream big enough that it will outlast you. Decide to express the fullest understanding of God's qualities that you know you have.

Here's another list of reasons why you may not be getting what you want:

• You are asking for something that you really don't want, but you feel that you should want it, or it's something that you used to want.

• You have a hidden fear of the responsibility of getting it.

• You already have it but don't see it, as it doesn't fit into what you believe you deserve, or the package it came in looks different from what you expected.

• You succumbed to an underlying pessimism in your thought, or you accepted an outside influence or belief as reality.

Whatever we are asking for must be in line with our expression of God. We must ask with boldness, ethics, and clarity, and then take action.

Lying

God dwells in you, as you. Everything is a manifestation of that. When you finally realize that, you can't lie to yourself. When you're part of a negative thing—demeaning someone or denying them food or dignity—you know it.
—Charles Haid

What is lying? Lying is not telling the truth, as we currently know it. We do it all the time. We lie every day as part of our life. We stretch the truth, don't tell the whole truth, don't reexamine our thoughts and update them. We lie to survive. We lie to get. We protect our "glittering image" our small-i. This is the person claiming to be who we are, acting out, and arranging our life in ways that are not truthful to our Spiritual being. We call this our personality.

This glittering image can ruin our lives if we do not consistently reexamine what we are saying and doing. The "I" that is the expression of God does not need to lie to survive, because it is always overflowing with joy and grace. The glittering image must lie to survive and in doing so kinks the supply hose.

Every once in a while I take a day and really listen to what I am saying, writing, and thinking. I ask myself, "Is this true?" On one of these "lie examination days," I bought a Starbucks Frappuccino, a treat for the week, and went to board the L.A. Metro. On the way into the station, I casually glanced at a sign that had one of those big red circles over a food picture.

"Oh phooey," I thought, "I just bought this drink. It will be okay to drink it while I am getting the ticket, but I will just throw it away before I board the train." That is what I did. I gulped it, not really enjoying it because I had to drink it so quickly, and then threw the cup away as the train pulled in. Just at that instant, a huge Metro police officer appeared at my left shoulder. "Did you see the sign?" he asked. "No," I said. "Well," he said, "You can't drink in the station or on the train, but you can carry it with you to your destination." "Thanks," I said, and he let me step on the train without giving me the very expensive ticket.

I sat down and replayed the whole scene in my mind. I was shocked to realize how many times in a space of five minutes that I had lied—and lied well! First, although I had seen the sign, I didn't read it, so I couldn't follow what it said. Second, I tried to beat the system; whatever I thought it was, by drinking my drink before anyone saw me. Third, I told the police officer that I didn't see the sign at all. Fourth, I got on the train before I could get the ticket—smiling sweetly of course.

So we think these are small lies and not important? Yes, they are small but they are still important. All lies point to the need to hide from Truth because we are not clear that there is only One Loving Mind. They allow the glittering image that is hiding the real "I" to stay in power. The glittering image does not want to die. As we step into the Truth of who we are, it knows it will vanish. In moments of distress, this false self is saying, "Help me, don't let me die." There is no reason to protect or keep alive this false self. When it dies, we do not die—instead we begin to live the life we were meant to live.

We established this glittering image in order to protect ourselves. As we grow Godward, we no longer need it. Thank it for protecting you when you needed it, and then let it go.

We must tell the truth to ourselves about the kinks in our hose and our dreams. We also have to be careful about looking again at our current understanding of what is true. Hopefully, every day we have a clearer understanding. If we are still answering and living from yesterday's understanding, we are lying. Denial kills the essence of who we are. Without Truth, life will become and remain hell.

The first and only lie.

The reason good people suffer, is they think they are people.
—John Hargreaves

The devil tells us that all we see is all there is.
—Carolyn Myss

The devil can cite Scripture for his purpose.
—William Shakespeare

There is really only one thing that we have to combat. That is the belief that there is another mind besides God and this other mind has power. There is not an alternative power. There is only One Infinite Omniscient Mind. That fact does not leave even the tiniest bit of room for anything unlike God. The appearance of another power is the temptation to believe in duality. When we accept duality, we succumb to the temptation to believe that all that exists is just what we can see. We have given the tempter power. Take it back.

The Lord's Prayer asks God to deliver us from the belief in the evil one.

The world, our mirror, gives us symbols to help us understand this truth and to uncover the lie. We know that there is more to life than what we see. We cannot see the wind, or music. We cannot see love, honor, peace, and so on. We do see their effects, so we know they are real. We can also see the effects of knowing that there is only One Mind and that it is good. Watching for and paying attention to these symbols will lead us to Truth and Grace, which have no paradigm to limit or filter the infinitude of God.

The perfect kink remover: Gratitude.

The person who has stopped being thankful has fallen asleep in life.
—Robert Louis Stevenson

If your kink in the hose is not obvious to you, move on to gratitude. A grateful heart always starts the Unkinking process. Sometimes thankfulness is all that is needed to start and continue the flow. If you have ever been depressed, you know how hard it is to move to gratitude.

The part of you that claims to be who you are doesn't want to give up its mood. It gets something from it. Depression is always self-centered. The glittering image, claiming to be you, gets value out of the depression.

Take control of your thinking and your life. Begin a gratitude list. Thoughts have no power to stop your connection to your eternal Source.

The best cure for worry, depression, melancholy, brooding, is to go deliberately forth and try to lift with one's sympathy the gloom of somebody else.
　—Arnold Bennett

The fulfillment comes in the seed.

I am only one, but still I am one. I cannot do everything but still I can do something. And because I cannot do everything I will not refuse to something that I can do.
　—Helen Keller

Just as an acorn has all that is necessary within it to grow a tree, all Angel Ideas have all that is necessary already provided for within them. All God's paths have the preparation laid. If we find ourselves walking a path that seems barren, there are only two possible explanations.

The first is that is it not barren but we're blind to what is there, because of our state of mind.

The second is that the path does not lead us closer to God. In either case, shifting our perception to the Truth of who we are and what God is will immediately provide the "things" we need.

This Shifting will open our eyes either to the provisions for the path we're on, or to the fact that we must change to a road leading to Truth, on which we will be amply and abundantly supplied.

PRACTICAL UNKINKING.

Pick someone you like least and write a gratitude list of his or her wonderful qualities. I often do this exercise in The Shift® class, and it is really wonderful to see the results. There is usually someone in class who says aloud what the rest of the class is thinking: "I hate this person! How can I find something to be grateful for, and why should I?"

The first reason you should is that not forgiving is a huge kink in your personal hose. The second reason is we are all one with God, so keeping someone out of that circle harms us all. Do you need more reasons than knowing that blessing your enemy blesses you and them and the world?

How can you be grateful for something about a person when everything about that person seems so hateful? Take the quality that you like the least about this person and flip it to the other side. Is this person demonstrating incredible stubbornness? What a wonderful quality of loyalty this may be. Is he being cruel? Perhaps it is a cover-up for the love he feels towards what he is defending.

You do not need to agree with this person or condone the person's actions; you just need to find the wonderful God-like qualities this person has so carefully hidden from view, and be grateful for these qualities.

Even if all you can be grateful for is someone's sense of order because she ties bows well, you have started a wellspring of blessing both for you and for the other person. Can you live with that?

Even for our enemies in misery—there should be tears in our eyes.
—Charan Singh

It is in the silence of the heart that God speaks.
—Mother Teresa

I am grateful for the following wonderful qualities in _____:

1. _____
2. _____
3. _____
4. _____
5. _____
6. _____
7. _____
8. _____

Chapter Twelve: S: So Be It

Detachment—not attachment.

Not my will, but Thine, be done.
—Jesus Christ

After we have done all that we can, and there is
nothing more to do, we turn it back to God. Amen, So
Be It.

This is when we practice detachment, not
attachment. This is when we put our actions where our
mouth is—God First. If we have truly put God First we
know that what is good, true, beautiful, and pure will be
the result; or more accurately, we will have seen that God
is all there is, therefore all is already good, true, beautiful,
and pure. We will have relinquished our human will
to Divine Will. We will have let go of controlling the
results. We will have done this with gratitude, because we
are aware that our egos often blind us to the Truth.

What ties us to this ego is emotion. Our goal is to
release emotion, to let it go. This is quite different from
expressing emotion or withholding emotion. Correct
releasing never has a negative impact. True releasing
allows us to open our hearts more fully and to express
and receive more love.

Lester Levenson of The Sedona Method has a
wonderful technique for releasing emotion to achieve the
state he calls imperturbability, which is the characteristic
quality of one who is self-possessed and not easily
disturbed or perturbed. This is the state of equanimity,
calmness, and composure.

He states that all emotions culminate in the following nine: apathy–grief–fear–lust–anger–pride–courage–acceptance–peace. In other words, after identifying the emotion we are feeling, we will be able to see that it is really one of these nine emotions. The Sedona Method takes us through the exercise of asking ourselves what emotion we are currently feeling, acknowledging it and then releasing it. We may ask, "Why let go of the wonderful emotions? "

There are two reasons. First, we must rid ourselves of the lifelong habit of holding on. We must let go of the thinking that whatever we have is as good as it gets. We are afraid to let go of what we have because we worry that we might not get any more.

This habit shows up in many parts of our lives. For example, it could show up in overeating because we are afraid that if we don't eat now we might not have food later. This symptom gets worse while dieting (die-ing). We might also notice this holding-on habit as it applies to other areas of our life like relationships and money. We'll cover more of this in Section Three on Relationships.

The second reason for not holding on to emotions—even wonderful ones—is that in declaring some emotions good, and some bad, we have also declared that there is both good and evil. This may be true in the material or physical and even the thought world, but not in the Spiritual. We desire to enter the State of Grace where there is only One Mind and that Mind is Perfection. The skill of learning how to release emotions plays a vital part in awakening to Truth.

Ask yourself, or have someone else ask you, the four questions at the end of this section.

As you do the Sedona Method exercise, you will begin to feel the emotion lighten. Often tears and laughter accompany the release.

This is a great spiritual muscle-strengthening exercise and can be practiced anywhere and anytime. The joy that bubbles to the surface as we relinquish all to God is enough to make us want to learn how to release or relinquish and say So Be It more often.

You may be surprised, as I have been, how often question three prompts a "no" response from yourself. Keep asking the question until you get a "yes."

In the end, we learn that all emotions resolve into only three wants—approval, security, and control. Don't these three sound just like our small-i ego?

Ask yourself:

1. Feel the now feeling.
2. Could you let it go?
3. Would you let it go?
4. When?

A suppressed emotion is one that we have pushed down into the subconscious part of the mind and we have become unaware of it Just know that they are there, and let go of them.
—Lester Levenson

The dance of completion and change.

Why is it that we put off completing things? Everybody knows the inertia of not making the one phone call or visit to the one person he or she really wants to call.

I can remember putting off for months calling the "quality client list" I had as a stockbroker by keeping myself busy with other clients and administrative tasks.

What are we afraid of—that they will say "yes" or that they will say "no?" Perhaps we are afraid of the completion—because completion means we must and will change. Not completing is a passive form of control.

I visited Hawaii many years ago on a business trip that stretched out to two months. I fell absolutely head-over-heels in love with it. At the end of two months, I had to leave. I felt that what happened was due to circumstances "beyond my control."

I missed it so much I could hardly stand it, and tried to make plans to return. However, something always got in the way. I chose to let circumstances and people keep me from returning. Always in the back of my mind I thought, "If it weren't for _____ (fill in the blank) I could live in Hawaii."

Eleven years from the month I left, I returned for a visit. Note this: it took me eleven years just to go back to visit my favorite place in the world—sound familiar? Nevertheless, taking that first step and saying to myself, "I am visiting no matter what. I am not waiting any longer for the whole world to fall in place before I can move back. I will simply visit and not worry about living there," finally got me on the plane.

After making that first choice towards completion, the rhythm of my life became more graceful and abundant. The next year I returned twice for a visit.

For twelve years, I had kept part of my life on hold thinking that if "things" weren't in my way I would live in Hawaii.

As I returned for the second visit, I had progressed enough to tell myself (and believe it): "You can live in Hawaii if you want to."

On the first day back I loved it even more than I remembered—and at the same time realized I didn't want, or need, to live there.

Since I was no longer blaming other people and circumstances for not being able to live in Hawaii I could see clearly that my desire was based on not completing my first visit, and thinking that something was taken from me, "outside of my control."

I still want to visit Hawaii as much as possible, but it is no longer necessary or desirable for me—my choice—to live there.

It is like shopping. Have you ever thought to yourself that you really, really, really want new clothes (I know guys, you might not want new clothes, go with tools or something) so you put the money together and go shopping saying to yourself, "You can spend this money on anything you want" and then realized there was nothing you really wanted to buy?

The desire to have what we think we can't have gets in the way of living our life.

Sometimes we think we want a relationship we thought we lost, or someone who doesn't desire us. Or we want a new job, or a new place to live. Not completing what we need to do in regard to any or all of these "wants" is a fabulous way not to live our life by blaming circumstances "beyond our control."

My completing—by taking action—my desire to move to Hawaii and then realizing that it was no longer my desire, opened a brand new door towards what I can choose now.

This is because once something is completed we can move on. It may mean that we do get what we thought we wanted, and it may mean that we realize we don't want it after all. The result is not what is important; what is important is that we complete something, and in that completion, we will find freedom.

For me, this completion means that I can now change my mind and decide to live there after all—or not—but it is my choice. I can stop blaming people, places, and circumstances for not doing what I want to do.

Everyone has uncompleted tasks, agendas, and desires. No matter how small they seem they are important. They are stopping the natural rhythm and flow of our life. When we straddle the fence of incompletion nothing can happen. Once we get off the fence, and begin to take the steps necessary to complete the task, life dream, phone call, book, picture, dream house, dream life...circumstances and events rush in to help us.

Change is inevitable. Change is going to happen whether we desire it or not. Best to make change a personal choice than change that results from having to fix things after the wake-up call that results in broken relationships, accidents, and illness—the list is endless.

In fact, nothing is ever the same from one minute to the next. Try looking at something and then moving just one foot away and looking again. Does it look the same? No. Personal perspective always determines what we see, and personal perspective changes every moment. Change is always happening. We just pretend that it isn't.

The truth is it takes more effort not to complete and change than it takes to let completion and change happen. Not completing and changing is hard work.

Trying not to change is like standing in a flowing stream and trying not to move. How can it be done? We have to hang on, make ourselves heavy, become rigid, and so on. Completing and change takes faith and courage, just like letting go and flowing with the stream, but it is simple once we start. Completing will bring with it a wave of fresh insight and energy and unlimited new blessing we never thought possible and the tools necessary to enjoy and benefit from the resulting change.

As part of the So Be It process, instead of making resolutions or setting goals, take the time to begin to complete just one unfinished dream or task. Don't waste time figuring out which one, just start somewhere. Take that small step and be ready to see the open doors that have been ready and waiting for you to walk through them.

It is the law of the universe to complete and move on, complete and move on, complete and move on. Each cycle is an ever-expanding one. Expanding and emerging is all that is happening. Be Willing. Pick your feet up, and dance with the music of completion and change. You will love the feeling of the dance, once you get started.

Start with the Spiritual fact.

Again, an error in the premise must appear in the conclusion.
—Mary Baker Eddy

Any apparent progress that results from beginning with the problem rather than the spiritual fact is a "dangerous resemblance". We can think our way out of problems. We can use our human will to make things happen. We can say, "The end justifies the means."

We can rationalize our actions. However, none of these ways start with God First and with relinquishing our human ego. For a time the result may look the same, but this is a dangerous resemblance.

This resemblance to Truth will try to convince us that we did put God First. However, some day in some way we will be confronted again with what we thought we had solved before, and this time it will be worse.

When I am tempted to ignore Angel Ideas even on a small scale, like not returning the extra penny change, I ask myself, "Are you willing to sacrifice your Life's harmony—Heaven—for this?" If my perception is on lack, how can my perception be with God?

As we awaken to Spirit's prompting, we discover the small and large lies we have been telling, to others and to ourselves. This is not the time to hold on to these lies through feelings of guilt, judgment, remorse or any other emotion that may surface. Here is the time to be grateful for our awakening and to begin to tell the truth, so that we can see more of the Truth. This is an ongoing process. It is a continual awakening, an upward and deepening path.

Another stumbling block to watch for is forgetting why we are Shifting. Once the physical evidence begins to appear, we may be tempted to be grateful for it rather than for the spiritual reality. Misplaced gratitude may open the door to ingratitude about what has not happened.

This is truly missing the point. We are not putting God First to get things. We are putting God First to be more conscious of who we are and to live in the harmony of the Kingdom of God.

Don't get comfortable—choose to keep going to the realm of no paradigm, where we are all with the One God, Living in the State of Grace.

Fly or die—the lesson of the dove.

Attachment is the greatest fabricator of illusions. Reality can be attained only by someone who is detached.
—Simone Weil

One of my first greeters in my new home was a pair of doves. For the year that I lived in my apartment on the canyon they constantly visited me at my feeders on the porch, or at the front door as I came home, or outside the bushes of my office. I thought they were wonderful. They were always together and always cooing. To me they were symbolic of my new love relationship.

I was overjoyed when I discovered the female dove was making a nest in one of my planters on our porch in the spring of that year. The only thing that worried me was that we were preparing to move across the country and I wasn't sure what would happen to them and their nest when we were gone.

One day while I was in the office I heard a crash on my patio and when I went to investigate I found my lovely female dove lying on the porch and her companion on the ledge cooing frantically. He was trying to wake her up. I did too. I wrapped her up in something warm and waited for hours for her to revive. She didn't.

I was as heartbroken as her mate. I couldn't understand why this had happened. He mourned for days and then one day he had a new companion.

This made me even sadder as I could not understand why or how he could just move on.

I kept wondering what the dove had taught me. I would only shake my head and say, "I don't know". I was too involved in the grief of it and couldn't understand why it had affected me so deeply. It took many months before I was conscious of the dove's lesson and gift to me. I was sitting in our new house in another part of the United States with absolutely nothing familiar around me and I finally understood.

She had tried to stay—and it was important to go. There was a part of me that was holding on to not leaving what I had known for the majority of my life— symbolized by my lady dove building the nest. The new lady dove knew that it was time to find a new home. She and her friend did not come back to my apartment to live. I only saw them the first day they were together as they perched in the tree and said "good-by" to me.

This is all symbolic of course, as all lessons are. Now that I have let go of so many things I realize another part of the love lesson my dove friend was teaching me. It really wasn't that one dove died and another took her place. The idea of holding on had to die. The part of me that was holding on had to die so that the person I really am—could fly.

Whenever I notice that I am still holding on to some of "how things used to be" I think of my friend the dove and thank her for the lesson about leaving, and I thank the new lady dove for choosing to go so she could continue her life with her new companion and find her wings.

Detach and let go and let God be the activity of your life.

A man can do what he wants, but not want what he wants.
—Arthur Schopenhauer

PRACTICAL SO BE IT.

Would you like to practice detachment or
relinquishment on a practical scale? Try this following
exercise. It might be helpful to share this with a friend in
order to support each other in its completion.

Step 1: Make a list of what you do yourself to keep
your household and/or your business running during a
month.

Step 2: Agree to yourself to give at least three of them
away in the next month. Giving them away could mean
to stop doing them altogether, or it could mean hiring
or asking someone else to do it. There are many ways
of detaching. One of the first is to allow others to help.
Remember our goal is to express who we are, not to do
more to prove our value. Our value is innate because we
are the expression of the One Mind.

Step 3: After one month has gone by, make a list of
what you actually gave away. Remember the power of
habits? Perhaps you meant to give it away, or perhaps you
gave it away and then took it back. Pay attention to the
underlying reasons why you kept it or why you took it
back. Acknowledge yourself for what you gave away then
ask yourself why you didn't keep your agreement with
yourself if you didn't. Observe the emotion; let it go, and
then do it again. You may discover that something you
gave away is something you really love doing.

It's okay to take it back if that's the reason, but be sure you choose something else to give away in its place.

This giving away can also involve physical objects that take up space and time. If you feel like they own you or that you are hoarding for the "just in case" moment, think about detaching from them. Remember thoughts are things. Go back to the quality you are trying to experience by owning these things and see if you still need the objects.

What's the purpose of this process? To practice giving up the lifetime habit of holding on. To begin to tell ourselves the Truth about who we are and what we desire. To begin to simplify our lives so that we have the ability to see the world differently.

Here is an agreement form for you to sign, to prompt you to act from "Not my will, but Thine."

I, _____, am willing to let go of my dreams and goals as I have stated them and allow them to develop through the One Mind. I am willing to put down the burden of making it happen or of being responsible for it not happening.

_____
Signature

I am giving away these three things I now do myself:

1.

2.

3.

What I actually gave away:

1.

2.

3.

What I am still holding on to:

1.

2.

3.

SECTION THREE

Walk Your Talk

Chapter Thirteen: The Relationship With Ourselves and Others

The Sixth Step To Shift—Walk As One.

Remember the game we called the Earth state of mind? In the Earth game we must overcome the belief of lack and at the same time be in harmonious and balanced relationships.

There is nothing we can do, think, or say that is not about a relationship. Truth is practical; therefore our expression of Truth will be practical and useful. We apply and use the Truth in every relationship we have, including with our bodies, our supply, our work, and our loved ones.

Relationships we have and the ones we want.

But relationships are not outside—they are inside of us; this is the simple truth that we must recognize and accept.
—Shakti Gawain

All relationships are really a relationship with ourselves. It looks as if we have relationships with family, friends, money, things, and our body: everything "outside" of ourselves. However, in reality all these "things" are within. As we work on peaceful and productive relationships of all kinds, we are doing the work on our point of view about how these aspects are supposed to behave.

Let's take a look first at our relationship with others, knowing that it is, in Reality, a relationship with our self.

Relationships are subjective states.

Relationships are subjective. What does this mean? It means that it is impossible to see other people as they truly are, because we are always filtering and layering in our own interpretation of them.

Pretend you're walking down the street watching someone walk towards you. At first, since the figure is far away, you decide that it is human as opposed to a dog or cat. As it gets closer you determine that the person is tall or short, fat or skinny, graceful or not, male or female.

Closer still, you may have determined the person's approximate age and possible nationality. With each of these determinations, you have made interior judgments based on what you know and have decided about each criteria. Of course, this is a short list. We place people in many more slots than this, all with preconceived ideas attached.

Once the person reaches you, perhaps you choose to meet them and you stop to stay hello. Assuming that this leads to a friendship, can you ever say that you really know this person? What did you predetermine before you met? We barely know ourselves. How can we really know another?

Communication

The concept of "Mondegreen" or the idea of mixing up words so that what is said is not what is heard can often be very funny.

However, the concept of word mix-ups is symbolic of how difficult it can be to understand each other. How many times in a day is there a misunderstanding.

Sometimes it is a simple misunderstanding that seems to harm no one. Other times this misunderstanding leads to major consequences that may take a long time to heal. Nevertheless, all misunderstandings eventually result in a feeling that all of us have had at one time or another, the feeling that "no one understands me."

It is so easy to misunderstand. Many years ago, I was preparing for a date with my boyfriend. I had carefully planned my outfit, but was still worried about it because it was a new "look" for me. As we were going out the door he said, "Boy, you look hot." I thought he meant I had too many clothes on for the season. I was devastated, and very hurt. After a brief pause to take in what he said, I asked him "Do you mean I have too many clothes on?"

He was amazed how easily I had jumped to the wrong conclusion. He of course meant I looked—well just as I wanted to look. We both laughed. What if I wouldn't have asked him what he meant? What if I had brooded all night about my appearance? What if I thought he was rude for saying such an unkind thing to me?

This is what we do, isn't it? We have our own point of view or perception about something—anything—and that colors everything we see, hear, or say about that concept. Do we really hear anything but our own point of view? Perhaps it is true, no one understands anyone.

Is this true for you? What could you do to change it? What could we all do to be in more harmony and balance with each other? Here are some practical things we can try.

• We could stop and pay attention to what we are thinking while we are listening. We could ask ourselves the question, "Am I listening to what is being said, or am I listening to myself comment internally about what I think is being said?"

• We could care more about the outcome for the other person than for the outcome for ourselves.

These ideas will work, and we can all practice becoming better at human communication. At the least, we could learn to laugh at those misunderstandings that do happen rather than taking them too seriously. However, there is a more effective, faster, and permanently better way. We could change our perception to something that would really clear up misunderstandings and would eliminate forever the feeling that "no one understands me."

In the Earth game there is a huge mist-perception. We think we are all separate from each other, with many points of view, many needs, many pains, and many agendas. If we would step out of the game and know what Divine Mind knows—that we are all part and expressions of Love and Truth—then all mist-perceptions and their ramifications would vanish. They would disappear as easily as fog lifts in bright sunshine.

Dissolving conflict.

I have learned through bitter experience the one supreme lesson to conserve my anger, and as heat conserved is transmitted into energy, even so our anger controlled can be transmitted into a power that can move the world.
—Mahatma Gandhi

Treat people as if they were what they ought to be, and help them to become what they are capable of being.
—Goethe

Sometimes we have people in our life with whom we have a conflict. This conflict can be the main source of the relationship or just a minor part of an otherwise harmonious experience. What can we do to either correct the conflict, or when necessary, extract ourselves from the relationship?

A productive way to resolve conflict may be to explain our feelings to the other person. If she or he is receptive and interested in evolving both personally and in the relationship with us, this may dissolve the conflict and move our relationship to higher ground.

However, sometimes this doesn't work because the other person is not interested in working with us to resolve the conflict. At this point most of us make the situation worse by focusing our emotion on the problem. This, we already know, only produces more of the same. Sometimes we really make it worse by bringing the other person's attention to the (our) problem with them. If the other person didn't already have conflict with us, they now do.

There is another way to dissolve that always works, if we are willing to detach from the outcome. Let me give you one example. I once had two relationships in my life where I felt I was doing all the giving and the other person was doing all the taking. They looked to me like they were people who thought of themselves first (and if asked would agree that they did), which left me feeling as if what I needed came second.

I was in personal conflict with both of these relationships because of my feelings of not being heard or taken care of.

They were both very important relationships. One was my husband, one my business partner. I resisted doing anything at first, as I was afraid of the consequences. Then I tried talking to both of them, but this only produced more negative results.

However, I began to realize that to heal the situation and to bless us all; I would have to see them and myself in a new way. I had tried this method before in other relationships and it worked like magic, most of the time in ways I would not have consciously chosen.

Looking back, if asked, I probably would have said that I thought the outcome would be that my husband and I would move towards a more intimate and mutually loving and satisfying relationship, and my business partner and I would separate. I figured she would leave the partnership, leaving me with our other partner, and of course, I just knew that both these things would be best for everyone.

When I recognized the pattern of my thinking and what I perceived as my husband's pattern of thinking, I did two things. I made a qualities list of what I felt a true loving relationship would embody. Once I did that, I realized that my husband was not really displaying most of those qualities in our relationship at that time. I began to question whether I was truly in a love relationship. However, I continued to see both him and myself as we really are—the expression of Divine Love—and to act out of that understanding as clearly as possible.

The result was not at all what I expected. Our relationship became more and more strained.

The more I attempted to do what I felt to be loving the more he pulled away from me and the more I felt his anger. It became apparent that he was not acting from love, but from fear. I continued holding to God's qualities for both of us as best as I could.

The result was that one afternoon I learned of a secret that he had been hiding and lying about for years. After a few days of shock and grief, I was able to feel great compassion for him, but I was not willing to continue the lie and live as we had been. I asked him to leave so we could begin to rebuild our relationship on Truth. This request he accepted by leaving, but never returning.

To my great surprise, in spite of the grief, I realized that a huge weight had been lifted from my shoulders and I was now free to take bigger steps towards the calling I was feeling.

As time went by, I was also able to see my own role in this failure. By continuing to hold to the truth about myself, I finally saw the lie that I had been living. I had lived a duel life. Somewhere inside of what I considered a very independent and capable woman, another woman had been hiding. This woman lived with the belief that she had to have a man in her life before she could do anything. When one man moved on, she focused all her attention on getting a new man. I knew this woman inside me did this. It was quite clear that I had to have a man first before I could get on with my life. I just never questioned the reason or wisdom for this decision.

Now I saw what had happened with all my romantic relationships. I would use my clear focus to find the man of the moment and fall in love. What happened next really wasn't the man's fault for he did not really know me.

He knew the "other woman" who had to have a man in her life. Once the home front was secure, I would emerge. However, in order not to lose the man the other woman had secured for us both, I paid the price of taking care of him. I gave him whatever I thought he wanted hoping he would be so grateful he would never leave.

Obviously, I did not think that I was lovable enough, so I had to bribe him to stay by giving him what he wanted, usually at the expense of what I wanted. Eventually, I would wake up and notice that I was doing all the giving, and the man would wake up and realize that the woman he fell in love with was not the real me.

After my husband left, I began to live my life, feeling and living from the strength and independence I'd always had. I did not look for a man to complete me. A few years after this experience I met a man who also did not need me to complete him. I continue to focus on being who I am, and this man in my life knows and loves the real me.

The business partnership had a different outcome. Once again, I made a qualities list of what I thought a partnership looked like. I began to act out of this, I thought, and began to see her as an expression of Divine Love. Now, this is the partner that I wanted to go away, remember?

Instead, she stayed and I became unhappier. The more I looked at divine qualities the worse our relationship got. The more I tried to step outside of the role of giver, the worse I felt.

One day I realized, finally, that the problem was within me. I was unhappy over her actions, because I was not doing what I really wanted to do.

She was doing what she wanted to do, and I wasn't. I had diverted my attention to a business that in my heart I knew I would have to leave. Instead of facing this, I focused on my partner's actions, so that everything she did mattered to me.

I changed. I stopped caring about the outcome. Although I did continue to hold to a principle of fairness, I started paying attention to my inner voice, which was telling me that I was not following my soul's path. I knew that I was diverting myself by worrying about a partnership and business that was no longer serving me. I began to tell the truth to both my partners. The result was that the "difficult one" became a friend and ally. We all agreed to a fair solution concerning the partnership that has blessed us all.

Nothing had changed but me. The world outside shifted with my personal shift to Grace. I had to give up being right. I had to give up caring about the outcome. I had to start being kind to myself first—rather than putting others first and then making them wrong for it. The process was only painful when I held on with fear to what I thought I was losing, or when I made myself feel guilty for my role in the past. Neither of these two emotions could bless me or the others involved. I reminded myself that I have always been the expression of the Infinite Loving One, and they have been too. Nothing had ever changed or could ever change that fact. The rest was a story we had lived out and from which we had awakened.

Did I ever tell either one what I was doing? No. I held in my own thought both their Divinity and mine—and acted out of that Truth. I used the GRACIOUS model to shift to Living in Grace.

When we see men of a contrary character, we should turn inwards and examine ourselves.
—Confucius

Why did this technique work for me? Most importantly because I put God First. I followed the GRACIOUS steps.

First, I tried to know, love, and see both my partners as God (Love) does. Next I Repented and changed the way I was thinking. This process demanded of me to listen for Angel Ideas every time I was disturbed by a situation and to go back to Love. I Chose for all of us to have a happy and productive outcome. I Imagined how happy we would all be and were, because we were living in God's Grace.

Of course, I had to keep it up, and be Obsessive about this Shift as my bad habits continually took me back to being upset.

I Unkinked my hose as I held to what was good, beautiful, true, and pure about all of us. I noticed many things that were not good, beautiful, pure, or true about myself and I let them go. I took action, seeking the best way to approach what needed to be done. And finally, I said So Be It and detached from the outcome. All these steps followed effortlessly because I started with God First.

I always prefer to believe the best of everybody—it saves so much time.
—Rudyard Kipling

Let your people go.

Love is like quicksilver in the hand. Leave the fingers open and it stays. Clutch it, and it darts away.
—Dorothy Parker

Often there are people in our life that we love who just aren't going where we are going. For reasons of their own, they have chosen a different path. If you see them as they really are they may choose to move out of your life rather than face the perceived discomfort of growth. Do not go back and get them. Do not drag them forward. Both of you will lose your focus on putting God First and you may end up staying with them instead of fulfilling your gifts.

There are unlimited paths to the One Truth. Each of us must walk our own and in our own time. We are blessed when we travel together on the same path, but when someone chooses one different from yours, bless that person, and move on.

Sometimes people take the path that moves them away from Grace. However, the wonderful story of the prodigal son reminds us that when one of our loved ones begins the path back of their own volition, we can run to meet him with a wholehearted love.

This is a time, once again, to put God First, not ourselves. For our small-i would like to remind that person of the pain we suffered while he was gone, and of all the sins of the past. But that is what they are—past. This is the time to continue to remind both you and the other person of who you really are, and let the focus on what is good, true, and beautiful become the basis of your life.

In all cases, we must tell the truth to ourselves before we can tell it to others. We will get exactly what we believe we deserve and expect. The Truth is we all deserve to be perfectly loved, and to perfectly love.

Find companions for life.

You deserve to be perfectly loved.
—Scott Peck and Shannon Peck, *The Love You Deserve*

Within each of us we house both male and female qualities. When we are in tune with our inner voice, we learn how to appreciate the value each aspect brings. As we value our internal male and female we will see in our outward lives friends and companions that fulfill these roles as well as completing these roles within ourselves…The female says, "I feel this." He says, "I hear your feelings. What would you like me to do?" She says, "I want that." He says, "You want that? OK, great, I'll get it for you." And he goes directly to get it for her, trusting totally that in her desire is the wisdom of the universe…Remember now that I am talking about an internal process in each of us.
—Shakti Gawain

The Chinese write whole words with symbols. In many cases, two completely unlike symbols are used to complete a meaning that is entirely different from either one of the separate symbols.

An example of this is found in the symbol for "Man" and the symbol for "Woman." When combined, they mean "Good." No wonder we have such a strong drive to bond with another—we desire a relationship that results in good.

However, many of us have not yet found the "one" companion with whom we want to spend the rest of our lives.

Consciously or unconsciously, we scan the horizon searching for "the one." Sometimes we meet the person who seems to be that one, but we find out later that although he or she may have been the one for that moment in time, that person did not wear well as we traveled together.

One way to filter out who is or who is not your companion is to look at the lifestyle that person desires. Does it match yours? Are you making a choice to be someone else, to live a life you would not really choose if you decided to choose this person as your mate? Our goal is to grow and expand our spirit, so choosing a lifestyle to buy affection will not accomplish that primary goal.

Are you not sure of even where to start in the process of finding a companion? Perhaps you could start with noticing who is attracted to you. Are they attracted to the essence that you want to be? Are the qualities you are expressing attracting the quality of the person with whom you might wish to spend your life? If not, choose the qualities that would attract you, and become those qualities yourself. Continue to ask yourself if you are living out of and expressing the values and qualities that you would like others to express to you.

Once we have found the right relationship, how do we keep it? To accomplish an ultimate rapport you must first find the values that you have in common. That means you must take the time to talk to each other, and to learn and share your values.

Once you each know the other, you can use the values you have in common to help with those that are not alike. The second step is to support and fulfill the other person's most important values as much as you can. This is the basis for a powerful, supportive, and lasting relationship, whether it is business, personal, or family. Of course, the opposite is true; if your values conflict there will not be harmony.

We must also commit to the relationship. The word commitment means "the agreement not to run." Although the word run conjures up a physical action like running for the hills, many of us run by withdrawing within our minds and hearts. The result is sometimes worse than physical running, since either party may miss the fact that he or she is now alone.

Another great danger to relationships is comparison. Nobody fares well when we are comparing him or her to someone else. The only comparison that works is comparing our thoughts with what the One Mind is thinking about a particular person, place, or thing (only good). Any other comparison will always result in feelings of unhappiness.

Human love.

Sometimes we pick the wrong life mates because we meet someone and for that moment in time they make us feel loved. But what if that "thing" they were doing that made you feel loved prevailed over all your other qualities and values? The other side of the issue would be, what if someone really loved you and had all the right qualities and values but was not able to make you feel loved?

In the first instance, you might end up with someone you would have never chosen, and in the second, you may lose the person who most loved you just because you did not feel loved.

How do we avoid this? Take the time to observe yourself and your relationships. Ask yourself, what about this relationship makes me feel like the person loves me? Of course, we can do this for all close friends, not just mate relationships.

I used this method effectively when I was dating and noticed that I kept being attracted to men whom I knew could not really be life mates. This attraction was the magnetic, when-and-how-often-can-I-see-you feeling. I stopped one evening and asked myself: "What exactly moves you to this feeling?" I discovered that there was a distinctive sound to the man's voice and the way he looked at me that would trigger this response. From that point on, those two things never grabbed me the same way again. Knowledge definitely is power.

Later, I again asked myself the same question. This time I wanted to know what really made me feel loved so that when I met my true companion I would be clear as to what I would need from him to continue to feel loved so that our love together would thrive over time.

This proved harder than I expected. I realized that I did not really know what made me feel loved because I had fooled myself so many times just to "get a man." To find out, I began to look at everyone in my life that I knew loved me (like my family and best friends) and then I asked myself, "Why do I know for sure this person loves me and what makes me feel loved?" I made a list of these qualities.

This was the list I used to filter out relationships I would have otherwise been caught up in.

Try this. It is a powerful and effective tool for finding and keeping true companionship. Of course, this is a reciprocal agreement. What do the people you love in your life—brothers, sisters, mother, father, children, grandchildren, mates, companions, friends—need from you to feel loved? Find out, fulfill it, and bliss is yours. In the end, it is Divine Love that we seek to express and experience. I had the following quote framed and hung on my wall, to remind myself daily what unconditional pure love acts like.

And now I will show you the most excellent way. If I have the gift of prophecy and can fathom all mysteries and all knowledge and if I have a faith that can move mountains, but have not love, I am nothing. If I give all I possess to the poor and surrender my body to the flames, but have not love, I gain nothing. Love is patient. Love is kind. It does not envy, it does not boast, it is not proud. It is not rude, it is not self-seeking, it is not easily angered, it keeps no record of wrongs. Love does not delight in evil but rejoices with the truth. It always protects, always trusts, always hopes, always perseveres. Love never fails. And now these three remain: faith, hope and love. But the greatest of these is love.
—Corinthians 13:1–8,13, Bible

PRACTICAL RELATIONSHIPS.

We often don't know what we want in our relationships because we've never stopped to consider the values that are important to us. Take your relationships one by one and determine what qualities and values you want. Don't think of a particular person, but a type of relationship.

The result of using qualities to find and keep relationships will bless everyone involved. Review the Chapter on God First to remind yourself how to make and use qualities lists.

The supreme happiness in life is the conviction that we are loved.
—Victor Hugo

In my_____ type of relationship I desire to be conscious of the following qualities:

1. _____
2. _____
3. _____
4. _____
5. _____
6. _____
7. _____
8. _____

In my_____ type of relationship, I desire to be conscious of the following qualities:

1. _____
2. _____
3. _____
4. _____
5. _____
6. _____
7. _____
8. _____

We do not great things; we do only small things with great love.
　—Mother Teresa

We should measure affection, not like youngsters by the ardour of its passion, but by its strength and constancy.
　—Marcus Tullius Cicero

There is no closer way to bond people than to align them through their highest values. Common values form the basis for the ultimate rapport. If two people have values that are totally linked, their relationship can last forever.
　—Tony Robbins, Unlimited Power

My greatest achievement in life—I made one woman supremely happy for 63 years.
　—Philip Carret, Pioneer Fund

It is more noble to give yourself completely to one individual than to labor diligently for the salvation of the masses.
　—Dag Hammarskjold

One of the deep secrets of life is that all that is really worth doing is what we do for others.
　—Lewis Carroll

We are all born for love; it is the principle of existence and its only end.
　—Benjamin Disraeli

Religion has nothing to do with compassion; it is our love for God that is the main thing because we have all been created for the sole purpose to love and be loved.
　—Mother Teresa

What you do may seem insignificant, but it is very important that you do it.
    —Mahatma Gandhi

Constant kindness can accomplish much. As the sun makes ice melt, kindness causes misunderstanding, mistrust, and hostility to evaporate.
    —Albert Schweitzer

Chapter Fourteen: The Relationship With Our Body

We are not in our body—Our body is in us.

There is no such thing as a material body: There is only a material concept of body. There is no such thing as a material universe: There are only material concepts of the one Spiritual universe.
—Joel S. Goldsmith, The Thunder of Silence

The human body is the outward expression of thought—just as everything else is—it is a purely mental product and objectification of material sense.
—Adam H. Dickey, God's Law of Adjustment

Our body is the outward expression of our thought. It is the holographic representation of our paradigm regarding our life, our parents, our culture, our age, and our belief about all of these.

Remember that a key element of Shifting is discovering the unconscious belief systems or points of view that filter all information to our consciousness. This rut, or paradigm, is what makes up our reality. What we conceive is what we perceive—and what we perceive is what we believe and ultimately receive.

This fact is easier to accept when we are discussing something less substantial than our own personal bodies. However, this truth cannot apply to one portion of our life and not to another.

Once again, we must remember that an error in the premise leads to an error in the conclusion. Always begin with God First.

If we remember to pretend that the Earth state of mind is only a game, then we can also pretend that our body is the marker on the board game of life—nothing more.

Trying to fix symptoms.

As I wrote this section, I was sitting in front of my computer with a bag of frozen peas tied onto my head. Why was I doing this? Because I was trying to deal with a symptom called a headache.

Besides being an incredibly silly thing to see, the cold from the frozen peas was assisting me in dealing with the pain while I wrote. However, I did not think the peas were curing the reason for the headache.

Come with me as we take a look at a few of the belief systems regarding our bodies and see if we can Shift our perceptions about them.

The story of the curse.

But there went up a mist from the earth and watered the whole face of the ground.
—Genesis 2:6, Bible

The first chapter of the Bible deals with the creation of the world as a Divine Thought. In the beginning was the Word. This is a clear description of a Spiritual Heaven present here and now.

In Chapter 2 (Genesis 2:3) we have another story of creation. We can tell it's a story because it begins with a mist coming up from the ground. This is the story of the mist-perception (missed perception) of Truth. If you have ever been confused, you know that it feels like a fog in your head (a mist). The ground, in this case, is the whole perception of Earth. We all know the story of being in Eden and then being quite efficiently asked to leave.

What went wrong? Why were we asked to leave? OK, Eve listened to a serpent. Perhaps we missed a few points when reading this story in the past. Did we notice that she must have talked to this serpent (i.e., suggestion) before, as she seemed quite familiar with him? There is no record of her yelling, "Honey, come quick, there is a talking snake in the grass!"

No, she carried on a conversation with him that she must have carried on before. She trusted him and didn't recognize the lie he was telling. The snake told her that God had said they could not eat of the tree in the garden. He told her what she wanted to hear. There is no record that they were told by God that they could not eat of the tree in the garden. The truth is God had told them that all that existed belonged to them. (Genesis 1:29) Eve had a conversation with the snake about something that God never said in the true record of creation.

What did the snake—or the suggestion of two powers—want Eve to do? Eat from the tree of duality. It is only in the second story—or the mist-perception— that the tree of good and evil, the tree of duality, is found. (Genesis 2:9, 17) God as Omniscience could not have known about another power. Omnipotence leaves no room for anything but Itself.

Eve succumbed to the suggestion that there was both an evil and a good world. Once she agreed with this point of view, and ate the apple, she perceived herself as belonging to a place outside of Heaven, and therefore she was. What we perceive to be reality magnifies.

Where do we want to Shift ourselves? Back to One—the concept that God alone is where we have always been. Since what we believe to be true becomes our reality, what better way to return to the Eden we actually never left—by choosing a God-First Reality?

Now, back to the story. Adam and Eve thought they heard God in the form of a voice that told them they were cursed. The voice could not have been God. God, being One, does not know duality. Adam and Eve were the ones accepting bad and good. God could not have had this thought, since God is Infinite Good. Perhaps it was the serpent? In any case, they felt cursed. The curse for women has been traditionally interpreted to mean that she will always be burdened with women-type troubles, and that men will till the earth forever (i.e., work) with no real satisfaction.

Since there was no truth to the first lie, there is no truth to this one either. Only the power we give to it! Defy this curse! God, as Infinite Love, could not curse Its own children. God as an Intelligence that is only Perfection could not have even noticed that they were accepting duality. No, the voice they heard was the same one we hear disguised as whomever we are willing to listen to, and often it sounds like our own voice. However, it is merely the voice of our personal serpent, once again claiming its power from its only source— the power we give to it. *What we perceive to be reality magnifies!*

We have readily agreed to this curse because we don't stop to think about its origin. We accept this script and play out the roles, not realizing that it is just a role, not Reality. Everyone knows that actors turn down scripts and roles that they do not wish to play. Turn down this limiting and abusive script—and any other script that limits your ability to live in the here and now Heaven of peace and harmony.

While we are observing the scripts we've accepted without questioning, let's look briefly at the script we've been given on heredity and genealogy.

Heredity and genealogy.

We are not the children of our biological parents nor did we create our own children. This concept is hard to grasp, but it's an important one. Of course, I can intellectually know that God is the Creator and therefore my children and I are all God's children. However, on a day-to-day basis I would like to claim that my dad is very brilliant and therefore I too must be, or that my mother is a fabulous, creative cook and so I am. Not to mention my children—how beautiful, handsome, successful, and talented they are—all of which I would like to lay claim to as their mother.

But if I succumb to this way of thinking, claiming myself as a child of humans, and a creator of humans, I also burden myself and my children with the other side of this claim—that of hereditary beliefs.

It is either true or not true that we are the expressions of the Infinite Loving One. We cannot carry forward any limiting beliefs about human personal heredity.

Choose the bigger gift for yourself and for the children who are your guests in this Earth game. Claim and act from the knowledge that we are loved by Love, which cannot include a limited reality. Of course as the reflection of Love we will do whatever is most loving to protect our guests and ourselves. When we start with the Truth of our being, Angel Ideas will lead us to the best solution for any problem

Aging

For us believing physicists, the separation between past, present, and future has only the meaning of an illusion, albeit a tenacious one.
—Albert Einstein

We do not die, we just change worlds.
—Chief Seattle

Most of what we experience in growing old is a result of a belief system that says we are supposed to age. Most of us have agreed to a decline in health the older we get. However, symptoms of aging are just that—symptoms of the disease called "old age." They stem from the belief that we live and die in our bodies. These symptoms are not required, necessary, or desired.

If there is actually no time—except of our own making—as physicist Stephen Hawking has stated, then why not stop measuring time altogether—especially when it comes to aging? We could start avoiding age-related thoughts by not celebrating birthdays as age related, which after all are simply measuring how many trips around the sun we have made. Instead, let's celebrate how much we've grown spiritually.

Watching our weight.

One of the first problems we have with weight is the mirror we are using. When I was in my mid-twenties I was taking a ballet class. It was my first class after having my third child and I was feeling pudgy. This feeling was not helped by the fact that reed-thin teenagers surrounded me. I was holding my own until I looked in the mirror.

Egad! I thought. Who is that really pudgy person? I could barely take the class as I dealt with fat feelings. I berated myself, I promised myself I would diet until I was thin. "Just please," I begged God, "don't let me be that person in the mirror."

When we moved away from the barre to begin center work, I was now looking into a different mirror. In this mirror was only a slightly pudgy me. One of the students saw my bewildered look and said, "Oh, don't pay any attention to that other mirror, there's something wrong with it and it's being replaced."

I had to laugh. Ever since, when I catch myself looking into a mirror, real or imaginary, I remind myself of that "wrong mirror."

The only mirror that tells the Truth about who we are is the mirror that shows us as God's reflection, whole, complete, and perfect. If I am surprised by what I see I say, "Thank God that is not who I really am!" I mean this statement in both ways.

Joel S. Goldsmith in his book *Invisible Supply* says, "Everything in your life is an expression either of your consciousness or your unwillingness to let your consciousness express itself.

When you block the expression of your consciousness, you become a blotting paper for the beliefs of good and evil that permeate the world. So you have a choice: you either become a blotter and take it all in and show it forth, or else you become a master of your fate and captain of your soul by an act of consciousness."

We are here to be the activity of God expressed in our own unique way. When we don't do this our body reflects the result. How long we procrastinate is up to us, but sooner or later we must respond to our calling. One common result (but not the only one) of choosing not to move in the direction of our dreams is the symptom of being overweight.

We must learn to trust Angel Ideas and take action towards our dreams. These dreams stem from our innate knowing of how we can express God best. Support what you believe and think with action. Remind yourself of who you truly are and ask yourself what mirror you are looking into.

The word weight really says it all doesn't it? What are we waiting for? What weight are we carrying? What heavy thoughts are we harboring? What are we waiting to do or be? Whom are we trying to please?

Whose rules do we follow? Do we listen to internal guidance on what to eat and when, or are we rebelling against what everyone else says we should do? When it comes to food, what unconscious things do we say to ourselves? What power have we given to food?

What words do you say to yourself about food? All the following statements will produce exactly what you say. Do you say any of them either aloud or internally?

- Everything good is bad for me.
- I can't trust myself to eat right.
- My body won't cooperate.
- I'd have to struggle and starve to have a perfect body.
- I'll never weigh what I want to because I am too old, too tired, I've had a baby, etc.
- My body needs to be controlled.
- If I eat even a little of this "bad" thing I will gain weight.

If any of you find that you accept any of these statements as true, stop now and begin to tell yourself the Truth. There is only One. There is only One of everything, including body. Therefore our body expresses now all the perfect qualities of God. Begin with the right premise—God First.

When we replace the untrue statements with the Truth, it may sound something like this: "I am the activity of harmony and balance. As God's activity of abundance, I have no need to hold onto anything. As an activity of Life's movement I express freedom."

These statements are not mere affirmations. They are Truth. Replace untrue statements with Truth, and you will never worry about weight again.

I have a friend who was burdened by the belief that if he ate a "bad" food he would, within seconds, weigh at least a pound more. I challenged him to prove it to me. We weighed him. He ate a cookie. He got back on the scale and weighed a pound more. Wow! Aren't we powerful beings? Our thoughts do produce the result we expect.

Challenge yourself to stop expecting and producing negative results. My friend and I talked about the truth, that the cookie had not produced the result, his thinking or point of view had kept him from seeing the Truth about himself and the cookie. What did the cookie represent to him? We decided that it represented love, and that Love could never harm him. The problem with food vanished.

Listen to your own personal self-talk about food and ask yourself what each act of eating represents. Choose wisely from what you learn and follow Angel Ideas into a balanced point of view. Then food will no longer be in control.

We are often tempted to have negative beliefs about ourselves that may kink our perfect-health hose. Review the following list and see if any of them sound familiar to you. These are some thoughts that may be going through your mind. Remember these are only temptations to believe that you are something other than the full expression of an Infinite Loving One:

Self-hatred / self-punishment / psychic protection / feeling too vulnerable / fear of being too sexy / fear of being too beautiful / fear of attracting too much attention / fear of being too powerful / thinking that weight equals strength / having a deep need for love / fear of expressing your creativity / fear of expressing your energy and holding it in / fear of emptiness / fear of having your life succeed so that you will have to give up your problems.

Do any of these thoughts tempt you to believe in their reality? Return to what is True. Follow the GRACIOUS line of reasoning. Start with God First, Repent, find another way to see what is happening.

Listen to Angel Ideas. Choose the result you really want, Imagine how you will feel with your perfect health and body, be Obsessively Vigilant while taking action in any way that seems appropriate to Unkink the hose, and when you have done all that you can, give it back to God—So Be It.

Exercise

For most people exercise is a way to fix a problem or to look better, which makes it hard to do. Exercise is neither of these two things, because there is no outside body to exercise. Exercise is a celebration of the Truth that we are already the expression of perfect health. This changes the whole picture. Instead of exercising to get "better," we exercise as the activity of perfection that is already who we are.

Angel Ideas will lead us to do something that feels like fun and is unique to us. They may lead us to the gym, or perhaps to the beach for a walk, or to take the stairs instead of the elevator. Exercise celebrates God's qualities such as action, grace, happiness, breathing, movement, and harmony. Design a plan that expresses who you are. Stop sitting on your "yes buts" and say "yes" to who you are. The result may look the same, but the motivation is entirely different.

Healing the body.

All disease is a breakdown in the relationship with yourself and others. It is a result of how you use your mind.
—Dr. Jacob Lieberman, Light Medicine of the Future

As I was writing this section of the book, a perfect instance happened to me that I would love to share with you so you can see how healing the body fits into The Shift to Spiritual Perception.

Remember the frozen peas on my head? Finally my headache abated, but I was aware of a lingering lack of energy and enthusiasm. Nothing I did relieved this symptom. The problem remained a mystery to me. A few days later, my partners and I went skiing. I had never skied before. I learned how to ski quickly and practiced a few times on the bunny slope.

The practice session went so well that I agreed to go to the top of the big hill and ski down, slowly, with my highly skilled partners leading the way. I really didn't want to ski down that hill and I felt that I had taken on more than I could do, but I managed to get most of the way down.

Near the bottom, I hit a very fast (for me) part and fell. At this point, I heard the Angel Idea, "That's it, you're done." I listened this time. I let the ski patrol come get me, and spent the rest of the day reading while my partners skied.

The next day I woke up unable to move my leg. For the first time ever, I took a taxi to work instead of walking the mile to my office. Now I had a symptom everyone could see and it hurt much more than my headache. I called my spiritual practitioner for help.

She reminded me that Divine Mind is unlimited in its motion. She asked me to forgive the moment and myself for what I was now considering a lack of good judgment. She asked me to take time to fully remember what was going on in the moment that I fell.

I realized that in that moment when I fell and thought I had been unwise, I was really only with God, reflecting perfect Intelligence and Grace. In Reality, the fall had never even happened—because God never conceived it.

The next day I woke up feeling much better. As I walked slowly to work, I reflected on how appropriate it was that I was moving so slowly since that was exactly how I felt in general. "Why," was still a question. I knew it had something to do with my dream of building my writing and speaking business. I had been staring at my work every night and accomplishing about a tenth of my normal output, and feeling no joy in the process.

This day I had a meeting with my business coach. Noticing my melancholy, he began to question me. The outcome of this was that I finally realized that the part of me called "Beca" was saying "no" to the dream.

She was saying no because it was just too overwhelming. She could figure out how to do each part, but the enormity of the idea as a whole meant that there were too many parts to do—and all she had was herself. I'd found the problem, and that was most of the work. Error uncovered is the beginning of the end.

I called my spiritual practitioner again. This time I told her about my lack of energy and the fact that I had also stubbed my toe not long before, so I had been hobbling for a few days.

As we talked, I realized that this had been going on for quite a while. My practitioner talked to me of Truth. She reminded me that God's plan carried the solution and that in essence I have never walked outside of that plan. The pain in my leg vanished immediately.

When I had first hurt my leg I thought I wouldn't be able to dance for weeks. I was able to take a jazz class the very next night.

I continued to think of the I Am—that I represent the Am in the Infinite Loving One. The mental fog lifted and I began to know how to carry out God's plan without worry about the outcome. The "problem" of feeling unable to move forward in life had dissolved and thus the symptoms—headache, stubbed toe, hurt leg, and melancholy dissolved as well.

PRACTICAL BODY.

How would you feel if you had the perfect body? Imagine, along with what your new feelings will be, and do the two qualities lists. Follow up with an I Choose page about body.

These are the qualities of how a perfect body "looks"—after putting the list in order:

1. _____
2. _____
3. _____
4. _____
5. _____
6. _____
7. _____
8. _____

These are the qualities of how I will feel—after being put in order:

1. _____
2. _____
3. _____
4. _____
5. _____
6. _____
7. _____
8. _____

I Choose:

I Choose:

I Choose:

I Choose:

I Choose:

Chapter Fifteen: The Relationship With Money

Waking up to the Money Fairy.

The only wealth is life.
—Henry David Thoreau

Have you been waiting for the Money Fairy? Have you been wishing on a star, hoping to win the lottery, waiting for your ship to come in? Do you look under your pillow in the morning, praying that the Money Fairy has been there?

Wake up! The Money Fairy is here, has been here, will always be here. Who is the Money Fairy? You, of course. She is the part of each one of us who is conscious and aware of the fact that wealth in all its forms is always immediately available.

When we listen to the Money Fairy within, we remember how to receive wealth. We remember that the money we need is the end result of understanding and living in true wealth, putting God First. She is the awareness that reminds us of Truth. She is an Angel Idea lighting the way to our innate wealth.

Are you as wealthy as you deserve to be?

Are you as wealthy as you deserve to be? Yes and no. Yes because you are as wealthy as your current paradigm says you deserve to be. No because wealth is unlimited, free, and always abundantly available.

Do you know anyone who is demonstrating this Truth all the time? Let the Money Fairy Angel Idea guide you from the small r reality of a limited point of view to the big R Reality, which has no limitations.

What is wealth?

Many wealthy people are little more than janitors of their possessions.
—Frank Lloyd Wright

What is wealth? It is not money. It is not possessions. It is selfless, flowing, unlimited love. It is grounded, safe, and secure peace. It is freedom from fear, worry, confusion, or pain. It is the ability to move, breath, dance, and sing without limitation. It is the unshakable awareness that no harm can ever come to you or to the ones you love. It is the knowing that you are loved and loving limitlessly.

This wealth is represented in many forms: companionship, love, shelter, peace, food, money, good health, and a secure future. When we wait for the Money Fairy, we are waiting for a representation of wealth.

When we awake to the Money Fairy within, we are conscious of true wealth. Thus, we see the representation or symbol. Most of us have it backward. We are working for the result and wondering why it is so hard to get rich (be wealthy).

Money is not required to buy one necessity of the soul.
—Henry David Thoreau

Each of us is a tree.

One of my very favorite symbols of true supply is the tree. Imagine with me a tree as it grows its first leaf. Do you think it worries that this is the only leaf it will grow? Is it afraid when its leaves start to fall off, or when someone harvests its fruits? Although we cannot hear the tree's "thoughts" we can easily imagine that the tree never feels lack or fear.

Instead, it "knows" its supply is not the leaf, the fruit, or the flower. It is what they are, their essence—symbolized as sap—that produces the outward symbol of supply. What makes it even more glorious is that those outward symbols bless so many other living things through their shade, their food, their beauty, and the purification of the air.

Next time we worry about spending a leaf, or harvesting our fruit, we would do well to imagine we are a tree and know that the supply within is God Itself.

What does the Money Fairy know?

The Money Fairy stands outside all paradigms. She knows Reality. The Money Fairy is always whispering in the ears of anyone who will listen. She reminds us, that there is a Higher Power, which is Mind, and that Mind is Love, the only Cause and Creator. How simple.

She knows that Spirit is substance, and that what look likes substance is only an outward manifestation of thought. She chooses to know only the One Mind's thoughts and she knows these thoughts are better described as ideas. She knows that ideas are wealth.

Do we know these things too? Of course we do, but we forget all the time. We are in the habit of living in small r reality. We forget that we have a choice. We can shift to the Money Fairy's point of view and begin to experience wealth. The Money Fairy does not deliver money itself, she merely leads us to the well that never runs dry, and sometimes the water looks like money.

The Money Fairy is always willing. She is willing to experience the unlimited wealth of Reality in all its forms. She says, "Yes!" to life. She lives her life in unabashed joy. Nothing can take her joy away. She knows it's the basis of being.

She says "No!" to restricted, unhealthy, selfish, or fearful thoughts. These thoughts do not exist in Reality. She says "yes" to ideas that are open, free, and loving. It does not mean she knows how the things she is saying yes to will happen. She only knows that in order to experience the wealth of Reality, one has to be willing.

We are often afraid to say yes. We make up very good reasons for saying no. We find friends who will agree with these reasons. We can usually prove we're right. But if we're not willing, nothing will change. We'll never find our way home to Reality. Our dreams will not come true.

Have you ever talked to people about a problem they're having, and you can see the solution clearly? You talk, explain logically, and maybe even get mad at them for not understanding. However, no matter what you say, or how hard you work to make them hear you, they just don't get it. They keep on saying no. They can't see what you can see. It's because you are outside of their paradigm, so the solution is obvious to you. They're inside of their belief system unwilling to let go to have things change.

Usually when we want something, it is not a big thing that stands in the way of having it. Usually it is a small, simple thought about which we're unwilling to change our mind. Remember the 1st Step To Shift is to Be Willing. No matter how badly we may desire improvement, or dream of having everything we've ever wanted, unless we are willing to have it, we will not.

How do we know what we're willing to have or to do? How do we know what our current belief system or paradigm is? We can look into our life-mirror. It will reflect back to us exactly what we think is true.

The world gives us direct, tangible evidence of who we think we are and what we think we deserve. This doesn't make us, or it, good or bad. It is just how we think things are. Wanting something better is the result of hearing the whisper of the Money Fairy—that there is more to life than what we call reality.

Sometimes we are not willing to change our point of view until many things happen to us that we do not like. Finally, we can do nothing more, and we whisper, "Help me." If we are willing, we will be helped. If we have moved ourselves out of the way; if we have said "I might be wrong about how things are;" if we have realized that we are not the One in charge; we will have become aware that we are the essence of God.

The endless I Am knows no limitations, has no judgments, no prejudices, no time. It is wealth. When we are willing to yield to it, our dreams unfold. If we have become humble and loving—we have become willing for the One Mind to guide our lives.

Our task is to get our human or small mind to consent to get out of the way. If the human mind could get better it probably would, but it can't.

All it can do is step aside and yield to the One Mind. Don't waste your time trying to change your mind—release it instead.

Do not wait; the time will never be "just right." Start where you stand, and work with whatever tools you may have at your command, and better tools will be found as you go along.
—Napoleon Hill

Focus on abundance, not lack.

To have and not to give is often worse than to steal.
—Marie Von Ebner-Eschenbach

All that we are arises with our thoughts. With our thoughts, we make our world.
—Buddha

Most of us, when faced with a problem, worry over it. We try all sorts of ways to fix it. One very important thing the Money Fairy knows is that if we are having a problem, such as not enough money, that is not the problem. We think it is. We focus all our attention on it but the problem gets worse.

We have already learned that a problem is a result, not a cause. It is a result of a choice, or a set of beliefs that we have in some area of our life. We know that where we focus our attention is where we get the result. In other words, it is our emotional thought that produces the result. For example, we can believe intellectually that we are all wealthy and that money is always available. However, when there's not enough money in the bank to meet our bills, fear takes the upper hand. Our emotion is a sense of lack.

Remember, what we believe to be reality magnifies, and it is emotion that does the magnification. Therefore, when we allow emotional fear to have the upper hand— we perceive more lack.

What is money?

Money, which represents the prose of life and which is hardly spoken of in parlors without an apology, is, in its effects and laws as beautiful as roses.
—Ralph Waldo Emerson

If money be not thy servant, it will be thy master. The covetous man cannot so properly be said to possess wealth, as that may be said to possess him.
—Francis Bacon

All achievement, all earned riches, have their beginnings in an idea.
—Napoleon Hill, Think and Grow Rich

Money is an object. Money is a representation of wealth. It is an object that can carry out a purpose without us being physically present. This object extends our love to everyone it touches as we express gratitude for its assistance in demonstrating that love.

When you spend money, are you thinking about gratitude and love? Or are you hoarding it because you think it is your wealth? If there is not currently enough of this object to accomplish what you want, do you let that perception become the truth for you? Does the outward picture become the inward?

Money is an emotion. We may think money is logical but it is emotional. As a Certified Financial Planner, I spent years listening to people asking me about their money. They all wanted to know the facts. What many were not willing to do was face the truth that facts have almost nothing to do with money. Money is nearly all emotion. Investing money with logic produces one kind of result. Investing money with feeling produces another.

Learning which emotions govern our spending gives us control. What we focus our attention on is what we will get. If our emotion is lack, lack will multiply. What we perceive to be reality magnifies—so Shift to true wealth and accelerate into abundance.

Money is a symbol. The weakest motivator is money—though you wouldn't know it to look at the world as it is today. We bid for the highest salary. We stay in work that we hate because it pays more. Companies offer money bonuses while treating employees as cogs in the wheel.

However, we must look deeper to find the real motivator. The only thing we can control is what we accept as Reality. Once we replace limited thought with God First our world changes. To be wealthy we have to stop thinking that we are working for money, and become aware of what we are really working for. Once we do that, we won't make the foolish choice of working twelve hours a day to provide for our family while losing them in the process.

I used to say routinely, "I want to be rich and famous." I couldn't understand why that wasn't happening. One day I realized that neither one of those statements was true for me.

I discovered I hardly cared about money, and could not get motivated by traditional ideas such as the being the biggest producer or getting the year-end bonus. And the thought of being famous actually scared me. What was going on? I was repeating what I thought was true, that we all want to be rich and famous. However, I had to find out what I really wanted.

There are four qualities money represents for most of us. These are *Security, Power (Prestige), Freedom, and Love.* When you have completed the worksheets at the end of this chapter, you will see where you spend your money— in other words, you'll know which quality motivates you the most. At this point, you can ask yourself, is this really what my work, or lack of work, is providing me? Am I working for money and sacrificing the quality? Which quality it is doesn't matter. It is the knowledge of what's important to you that makes the difference. Do the worksheets and find out for yourself.

One result of completing the worksheets is that you may find you have a value conflict. This happened to me.

Although I had been using these worksheets in my "The Truth About Your Money" workshops, I had not filled them out myself for years. While writing The Shift class I transferred the worksheets to class notes and decided to do them again myself. Since I was struggling with money supply at the time, I was willing to do anything to uncover what was blocking my progress.

The result showed me that freedom and security held equal place in my mind. We already know when we have two equal values, or qualities; our core-self does not know which one to give us. We have to put the qualities we want in descending order. At that point, we move forward.

I understood the value conflict immediately. Valuing freedom, my days were my own and I did not have to report to anyone. Valuing security, I wanted enough money to pay my bills and have enough left over to play.

However, in my case, at that time, putting freedom first meant that I was not secure; I did not have enough money to pay my rent or to play, and so I was not really free either.

I recognized that I had been ignoring the Angel Idea that had been knocking at the door of my mind for over a year—to return to the work I knew and did well (financial planning) and provide security for myself first. Then I could find freedom.

I realized that I was not being practical or loving to myself by continuing to struggle at something that could not yet provide for me. I was not going to give up my dream, I was just going to provide a measure of security in order to be free to create and think instead of worry.

During this thought process I discovered hidden fears about what would happened to my internal values, and my life, if I returned to the business world.

I confronted these fears by knowing that Love always provides a place for me to be myself and take care of myself. The result was much better than I imagined, and by returning to the business world I became more valuable to others as well as to myself.

Because I was clear about what I wanted to offer, at no point did I have to compromise what I believed in.

Working for all the wrong reasons.

Whatever your think having more money will give you—aliveness, peace, self-esteem—is the quality you need to develop to become more magnetic to money and abundance. View money and things not as something you create to fill a lack, but as tools to help you more fully express yourself and realize your potential.
—Sanaya Roman and Duane Packer, Creating Money

At any point that you begin to substitute money as a goal, as a motivating factor, for the more important things in your life, you may end up in pain.
—Michael Phillips, The Seven Laws of Money

I was talking to a couple about their desire to purchase a vacation plan that would last them through their lifetime and their children's and grandchildren's. We spoke about how much the children would like it, and how they might use it to travel more. While we talked, I questioned them about their family. It turned out they had five kids, but they rarely saw each other as an entire family, never had meals together, and the dad was feeling badly because he hadn't seen his oldest son for a few weeks. They were missing each other because of their schedules.

The dad worked a huge number of extra hours at his job. Why? The company requested it. He had just spent $14,000 for a tractor to mow his lawn. However, when the decision came down to purchasing the vacation package he turned it down. Why? Not enough time to take a vacation (he didn't want to disappoint the company) and he didn't want to spend the very small amount of money the membership would cost.

If he would have been willing to tell me what he loved most and the qualities most important in his life, I am fairly sure he would have answered—my family and their happiness. Yet, everything he did said otherwise. He was working for all the wrong reasons and missing the whole point.

Things that matter most must never be at the mercy of things that matter least.
—Goethe

Poor is a state of mind.

The majority of people who fail to accumulate money sufficient for their needs are generally easily influenced by the opinions of others.
—Napoleon Hill, Think and Grow Rich

Poor is a state of mind, broke is a temporary condition.
—Michael Todd

Poverty is a contagious disease. There is no value in being poor. Poverty is a sin in the real meaning of the word: We are missing the mark of who we really are and what we already have.

Don't accept the common point of view that there is not enough. We live in an agreed-upon perception, or paradigm, that idealizes a sense of lack.

Not just lack of money, but lack of time, lack of love, lack of patience, and lack of courage.

The news reports lack. Friends report lack. Advertisements want us to feel lack so we will buy their product. Break this cycle. Shift out of this low gear that grinds uphill and state the Truth.

As the expressions of the Infinite Loving One, we are already and always the expression of wealth. Since God is omnipresent supply—where is the lack?

Each of us has all we need in every phase of our lives. Make wealth contagious by listening to Angel Ideas, and then take action on the ideas and gifts they bestow.

Remember, to receive you must first give. However, be cautious. Don't give so much away that there's nothing left. This type of giving also causes poverty.

Unkink the money-hose.

When your money-hose is kinked and instead of a stream you are getting a trickle, ask yourself whether you are tempted by thoughts or ideas in the list below. All of us to some extent have one or more of these thoughts rumbling around in our minds. However, once we see through them they begin to dissolve. Remember, these suggestions are not our own thought, just temptations to believe in duality.

• Not understanding or acknowledging what is true value.

• Not understanding or acknowledging another's value.

• Being afraid that there is not enough.

• Remaining in the habit of "thinking poor."

• Harboring thought patterns such as hate, bitterness, and despair.

• Having feelings that the world owes you a living.

• Wanting it our way.

• Believing that we are separated from the Source.

• Believing that there is something else besides the One Mind.

- Believing that we are the creators—for good or evil.
- Not putting God First.
- Thinking that poor is a divine quality.
- Believing the misconception that to be wealthy people have to compromise their values.
- Not wanting to accept the responsibilities of wealth.
- Afraid of "doing better" than those we love.
- Believing in the role of our gender.

If there is not enough cash flow it may be because of one of the following reasons:
- Believing money is something we have to earn.
- Believing supply is an outside representation.
- Forgetting it's the product, not the purpose.
- Believing in the myth of lack—of all kinds.
- Stockpiling and not circulating. This applies to everything, including money.
- Not completely living up to our highest sense of integrity.

Once we uncover a negative thought pattern, return Back to One—to the One Mind. We do not claim these thoughts as our own. Relinquish and release.

Fear of poverty is a state of mind, nothing else! But it is sufficient to destroy one's chances of achievement in any undertaking.
—Napoleon Hill, Think and Grow Rich

The principles of the loaves and fishes.

As I have mentioned before, there is a wonderful story in the Bible that illustrates true supply, the story of the loaves and the fishes (John 6:1–14).

Instead of thinking that only someone as wise and as evolved as Jesus could accomplish this "miracle," let's look at what he may have been trying to tell us. What Laws of Spirit was he demonstrating?

Jesus was teaching a multitude, a crowd. He was so interesting to listen to that as he walked, the crowd followed. Towards the end of the day, Jesus realized that the crowd must be hungry. Love is practical. While teaching about eternal Love and endless supply Jesus did not expect the crowd to go hungry.

The disciples, thinking there was no way to feed everyone, told Jesus that he was not responsible for making sure they were fed. He had been teaching Truth all day, what more could he do? They suggested he send the people home to eat.

Since there was no handy-dandy fast-food restaurant nearby, Jesus thought that this would be unkind.

Love is indeed practical. Taking care of human needs while we learn of the Truth is both wise and necessary.

What happened next? Andrew, one of the disciples, noticed that a lad had a few loaves and fishes, but he was not sure how they could feed the crowd.

Jesus had no doubts. He did not believe what his eyes were telling him. For us this might translate into not believing the checkbook, but turning to God First.

When something looks impossible, we know it seems that way because we are seeing the situation through a material lens.

The story continues. Jesus thanked God for what He had already provided.

Three points:

• Jesus never doubted at that moment that he was personally provided for.

• He also knew that everyone in the crowd was already provided for.

• He was grateful for this understanding.

Once he received the loaves and fishes from the lad, Jesus had the disciples begin to feed the crowd. What points was he making? First, there was no time delay. The seeds did not need to be found and they did not have to wait for the seeds to grow to harvest the grain to turn it into dough and then bake the bread. There is no time factor in God's provision. Second, he expected and knew that Mind's (Love's) provision was always available and demonstrable.

The last point is one of my favorites. After everyone was fed, there was an abundance left over! Most of us operate from the belief system of having just enough to get by. This story demonstrates to each of us that we should expect to receive an overflowing abundance at all times. There is no waste. It is our heritage to have more than we need.

What is debt?

But by an equality, that now at this time your abundance may be a supply for their want, that their abundance also may be a supply for your want, that there may be equality.
—II Corinthians:8:14, Bible

Debt is a gift from someone who believed in you enough to lend you money. When you repay debt, you are repaying a gift. Our bills are a form of a gift. The utility companies provide light, water, and phones before we pay for them. What a gift! It is a belief in our future selves.

At some time, most of us either lend or borrow money. How we approach either side of this process either blesses us or kinks the hose. Each of us at different times in our lives has more to offer than someone else. Sometimes this giving does not come in the form of debt but through a wise business transaction.

When I first began in the financial planning industry, I sold life insurance. I had a great deal of trouble with the word "sell," because I didn't want to manipulate people into something they really didn't want to do. Eventually I learned that my purpose was to let them know what I had to offer as truthfully as I could, and then give them a safe place to make the right choice for themselves. This reasoning helped me through the first hurdle of selling.

One day I discovered another hurdle. I was in the middle of a divorce and really felt that I needed a life insurance deal to close so I could move my children and myself to a new home. I found I was afraid to close the deal. I didn't want to impose my own sense of lack upon the women I valued as a friend.

Then I read the quote above from Corinthians about equality and I saw the deal in a new way. I realized that at that moment, my friend's abundant money supply could provide what she needed in the form of life insurance, and I could provide that "right idea." It was equality. I was not less because I didn't have enough money. We were both blessed by the transaction.

If we approach the repayment of debt of any kind with the thought, "Oh no, I have to pay this," we are kinking the money-hose. If you have a debt that you do not want to repay, you may end up not receiving any money at all just so you won't have to pay it.

If you aren't receiving enough money and you have debt, ask yourself:

- Am I choosing to not pay?
- Am I withholding Love from anyone?
- Am I withholding forgiveness from anyone, including myself?
- Am I not expressing gratitude for the gift I have?

Here is one more thing to ponder. Before choosing to borrow, make sure that you are not using debt simply to escape what is going on now, while giving your future self a problem. Remember, debt is either a gift or a burden to your future self, so make sure you are borrowing for the right reasons.

Goodness is the only investment that never fails us.
—Henry David Thoreau, Walden

PRACTICAL MONEY.

Ask yourself, "What is wealth to me?" To get the wealth we expect we must keep our focus only on wealth. Be grateful for the overflowing abundance of ideas—true wealth—that supply us moment by moment. Don't forget that it is okay to expect and receive money as a form of wealth. List here your qualities of wealth and have a friend help you put them in order. (See the Chapter God First for a reminder on how to do qualities lists.)

Then do an I Choose sheet on what you want to see. The combination of a qualities list and an I Choose sheet is very powerful.

The qualities of what wealth looks like to me:

1. _____
2. _____
3. _____
4. _____
5. _____
6. _____
7. _____
8. _____

The qualities of how I would feel if I were completely wealthy:

1. _____
2. _____
3. _____
4. _____
5. _____
6. _____
7. _____
8. _____

I Choose:

I Choose:

I Choose:

Cash flow worksheets

Please use the following pages to track your expenses. Fill out the first column, labeled "Monthly Guessing" without looking at any source of information.

Fill out the second column "Monthly Actual" by looking at your expense records. Use checkbooks, receipts, taxes, etc. Note the difference between the two columns.

Use the third column (Annual) to multiply the monthly actual by 12 to discover how much money you spend each year on each item.

Note: The first part of this exercise (guessing) is designed to give you an idea of how much you do or don't know about where your money is being spent. If you didn't know, was it because you don't want to face it? If you knew exactly, are you trying too hard to control your money flow?

Just observe and answer the questions for yourself. If you are part of a couple or partnership, do these worksheets separately first.

The second part of the exercise is to find out what you are really spending. Telling the truth is the first step in making changes. However, do not be hypnotized by the numbers. Remember, they are only telling you want you currently perceive to be reality. Keep your emotions out of this exercise so that you do not magnify any problems you may be facing.

After you finish this part of the exercise there will be a final—third part—to discover why you spend the money where you do.

ITEM	MONTHLY ACTUAL	ANNUAL
HOME		
Rent / Mortgage		
Mortgage Interest		
Equity Line Payment		
Equity Line Interest		
Home Maintenance		
Dues and Fees		
Home Insurance		
TV / Internet		
Phones		
Utilities		
Yard Maintenance		
Home Decoration		
Property Taxes		

CARS		
Payments		
Payments		
Interest		
Maintenance		
Fuel		
Auto Insurance		
Fees & Licenses		
Vehicle Taxes		

ITEM	MONTHLY ACTUAL	ANNUAL
INSURANCE		
Life		
Health		
Disability		
Liability		
Long Term Care		
Extra		

ITEM	MONTHLY ACTUAL	ANNUAL
GENERAL EXPENSES		
Bank Fees		
Medical		
Dental		
Child Support		
Allowance		
Alimony		
Clothes		
Grooming		
Classes		
Reading		
Entertainment		
Groceries		
Eating Out		
Travel		
Vacation		
Gifts		
Moving		
Charity		

ITEM	MONTHLY ACTUAL	ANNUAL
School		
Kid's Stuff		
Fun		
Financial Advisor		
Life Coach		

CREDIT AND DEBT		
Payments		
Interest On Payments		
Fees		

SAVINGS		
Emergency Fund		
Long Term Savings		
Ira's		
SEP / 401k / 403b		
Other		

OTHER REAL ESTATE		
Rent / Morgage		
Mortgage Interest		
Dues & Fees		
Insurance		
Utilities		
Decorating		
Maintenance		
Property Taxes		
Marketing/Rent/Sell		

ITEM	MONTHLY ACTUAL	ANNUAL
HOME BUSINESS		
Entertainment		
Marketing		
Legal Fees		
Accounting Fees		
Financial Advisor		
Other Consultants		
Education		
Debt Payment		
Debt Interest		
Product Supplies		
Office Supplies		
Website Fees		
Computer Fees		
Non Reimbursed Employee Expenses		
Other		

	MONTHLY ACTUAL	ANNUAL
TAXES		
Federal		
State		
Local		
Social Security		
Other		

	MONTHLY ACTUAL	ANNUAL
TOTALS		

The third part of this exercise is to place the actual numbers in the following tables. Here's how: Take the annual total for each expense and place it in the column or columns that feels the most appropriate. (Some expenses are missing from this part of the exercise because they're irrelevant to the categories.)

For example: Pretend your rent is $12,000 a year. Look at the categories and decide that 50% of the money you spend on rent is because you want to feel secure. Enter either the dollar amount or percentage. That leaves you with 50%, or $6,000.

You look at the categories again and decide that 25% of the rent is based on wanting to live someplace that has prestige (power) and the remaining 25% is because you want to feel free where you live. Enter each number on the appropriate line.

When you are done adding the columns you will have a clear picture of why you are working for money. Does this fit with what you truly want?

ITEM	SECURITY	POWER	FREEDOM	LOVE
HOME				
Rent / Mortgage				
Mortgage Interest				
Equity Payment				
Equity Interest				
Home Maintenance				
Dues & Fees				
Home Insurance				

ITEM	SECURITY	POWER	FREEDOM	LOVE
HOME				
TV/Internet				
Phones				
Utilities				
Yard Maintenance				
Home Decoration				
Property Taxes				

ITEM	SECURITY	POWER	FREEDOM	LOVE
CARS				
Payments				
Payment Interest				
Maintenance				
Fuel				
Auto Insurance				
Fees & Licenses				
Vehicle Taxes				

ITEM	SECURITY	POWER	FREEDOM	LOVE
INSURANCE				
Life				
Health				
Disability				
Liability				
Long Term Care				

ITEM	SECURITY	POWER	FREEDOM	LOVE
GENERAL				
Medical				
Dental				
Child Support				
Allowance				
Alimony				
Clothes				
Grooming				
Classes				
Reading				
Entertainment				
Groceries				
Eating Out				
Travel				
Vacation				
Gifts				
Moving				
Charity				
School				
Kid's Stuff				
Fun				
Financial Advisor				
Life Coach				

ITEM	SECURITY	POWER	FREEDOM	LOVE
CREDIT & DEBT				
Payments				
Interest on Payments				
Fees				

ITEM	SECURITY	POWER	FREEDOM	LOVE
SAVINGS				
Emergency Fund				
Long Term Savings				
Ira;s				
SEP / 401k / 403b				

ITEM	SECURITY	POWER	FREEDOM	LOVE
OTHER REAL ESTATE				
Rent / Mortgage				
Dues & Fees				
Insurance				
Utilities				
Decorating				
Maintenance				
Property Taxes				
Market To Rent or Sell				

ITEM	SECURITY	POWER	FREEDOM	LOVE
HOME BUSINESS				
Entertainment				
Marketing				
Legal Fees				
Accounting Fees				
Financial Advisor				
Other Consultants				
Grooming				
Education				
Debt Payment				
Debt Interest				
Product Supplies				
Office Supplies				
Website Fees				
Computer Fees				
Non Reimbursed EE Expense				

ITEM	SECURITY	POWER	FREEDOM	LOVE
TOTALS				

Circle the highest column. This is the quality for which you are working. Do you notice a value conflict? Decide — at this moment — which is the most important value.

Chapter Sixteen: The Relationship With Our Purpose

The best effect of fine persons is felt after we have left their presence.
—Ralph Waldo Emerson

The questions, "Who am I?" and "Why am I here?" fly around the back of our heads and bang on the door of our minds. When we open the door, we can get interesting answers.

The ducks said stop!

We are put on this earth to reflect what is best about ourselves.
—Charles Haid, Drama-Logue

One time some ducks admonished me for not knowing the answer to these questions. It happened one day when I was running. I was going through a change of marriage and career and wasn't quite sure where I would go next. I got into the habit as I was running of asking myself "What shall I do? Who am I?" My running route took me by the harbor, where I would often have to pick my way through a flock of ducks. One day as I ran through the ducks I heard them say—really!—"You are driving us crazy with this question. Why don't you just be yourself? We never ask 'should we be ducks?'— we are just exactly what we are and we don't waste time wondering if we can be something else."

You think I didn't hear this? I did, or at least I knew that was what they were saying—and it stopped me cold. I realized the truth of what they were telling me. We all bloom as the plant that we are. I could care for myself as if I were a rose knowing I am a lilac, but I could never stop being a lilac. What I needed to do was just be who I am and take care of myself as that person—and stop pretending, or wishing, I was someone else. And that is all you need to do, too. That is your purpose, to express who you are.

I long to accomplish a great and noble task, but it is my chief duty to accomplish small tasks as if they were great and noble.
—Helen Keller

Our stumbling block comes into play when we think it matters how we express ourselves. When we think that some callings are more important than others, we may not think ours is important enough. That is far from the Truth. Each flower in the field, each duck in the harbor, each person is a unique and necessary part of God's expression.

As we listen to Angel Ideas, we begin to know who we are and what we love to do. This is the key, loving what we do. Let's do an exercise that may help us determine what we love and how we would like to express it.

Throughout this book, we have done many qualities lists so by now you're quite an expert. Take a moment now and review your lists. Make a new list of the top 8 to 10 qualities and values that you feel you must have in your life. For this exercise, they do not have to be in order.

The qualities and values that mean the most to me:

1. _____
2. _____
3. _____
4. _____
5. _____
6. _____
7. _____
8. _____
9. _____
10. _____

Now comes the fun part. Trust your inner voice to speak while you do this. In other words, get your logical mind out of the way. Take these 8–10 qualities and make them into not more than three sentences that describe you and your life. Be sure to include emotion and action.

What have you done? You have written a mission statement that can be used as a yardstick to measure your actions and decisions.

In The Shift classes where I use this, some people know they have written something wonderful, and others think they have written something less than wonderful. You know what? Everyone always writes something wonderful, because it gives a clearer picture of the heart, and the heart is the first place to begin your life and purpose.

In the fabulous movie Pleasantville, as the inhabitants expressed an inner value of their heart they each transformed from black-and-white to full color.

The hero stayed black-and-white until he expressed the value he thought he most lacked—courage. When he expressed it through a selfless act, he discovered it had existed within him all the time, just as you will.

Becoming yourself.

You have certain mental images of yourself, your world, and the people around you, and you behave as though those images were the truth, the reality, rather than the things they represent.
—Maxwell Maltz

We use electricity every day. Have you ever stopped to think that when we plug in a lamp it is the lamp that "decides" how bright it is going to be? The electrical wiring in our house doesn't know of the lamp's choice. It could be a 20-watt bulb or a 120-watt bulb. The electricity is just being electricity. The lamp is expressing the electricity; otherwise, we would not see it.

We are like lamps. We are all connected to the Source of One Infinite Love. How bright we choose to shine is up to us. Why not choose to be a 120-watt bulb?

In his famous "I Have A Dream" address in 1963, Martin Luther King Jr. said, "In a real sense all life is interrelated. All men caught in an inescapable network of mutuality, tied in a single garment of destiny. Whatever affects one directly affects all indirectly. I can never be what I ought to be until you are what you ought to be, and you can never be what you ought to be until I am what I ought to be."

Meeting obstacles.

Ah, it seems so easy. Just plug into the Infinite Mind and express It through our illumination. Why don't we? What seems like a difficult question has a simple answer. It is because we believe that we are human, and acting out of "human nature," instead of knowing we are Spiritual.

Easy not to do.

> *The reason people fail or wallow in mediocrity is not because of what they don't know—it is because they refuse on a daily basis, to put into practice the things they do know. The natural inclination is to gravitate to the line of least resistance. That which is easy to do is easy not to do!*
> —Matol Training Handbook

When I was in my twenties, my mentor tried to tell me why people wallow in mediocrity. I would nod wisely at her and think that I understood. Only recently have I really understood what she meant. It is our "human nature" to think life must be hard. When we were growing up there were things that we did that came very easily to us. We loved doing them. Somewhere we decided that since they were so easy to do they must not be important. Definitely they were not how we were going to "make a living" because "making a living" was supposed to be hard. For most of us, the easy thing to do slipped away. It was even easier to let them go.

This also pertains to not doing what we know how to do. We already know how. However, our small mind says, "Well then, there must be more to know." Doing what we know would be too easy and therefore no longer important.

The key to loving our life purpose is to take back the easy thing. Go back and find it, and then move forward with what you love to do. Shifting may sometimes be uncomfortable, but not hard. Doing what you love may make you uncomfortable, but it will feel joyful. Take each day and do something you already know how to do. It really is easy to Shift out of low gear into high gear when the car—you—is moving!

It seems to me that those songs that have been any good, I have nothing much to do with the writing of them. The words have just crawled down my sleeve and come out on the page.
—Joan Baez

What will people think?

The reasonable man adapts himself to the world; the unreasonable one persists to adapt the world to himself. Therefore all progress depends on the unreasonable man.
—George Bernard Shaw

What does it matter what people think? People will think anything they want to, no matter what we do. They will misquote and misunderstand us even when we do the best we can to fit into their paradigm. Given that, why not be doing something that makes you happy? It will surprise you how many wonderful new friends you will make who will support what you are doing, once you begin. What people think is their business, what you do with your life is yours.

Breaking habits.

The secret of success is constancy of purpose.
—Benjamin Disrali

No one can possibly achieve any real and lasting success or get rich in business by being a conformist.
—J. Paul Getty

A foolish consistency is the hobgoblin of little minds.
—Ralph Waldo Emerson

Hello—isn't this crazy? We hang on to "less than best" just because we know what it looks like and how to deal with it. Crazy but true! We know what our life looks like now. Why change? We hold on to cars, relationships, and lives that aren't working, because at least we know how they don't work. We can adjust to fit into what will happen, when we get home or start the car, because it happens that way all the time.

Change is the universe's request to stretch and shift. Either you will follow the gentle request, or it will begin knocking and then pounding, until one day you finally wake up and begin expressing your unique version of the Infinite Loving One. After all, look what happened to Jonah when he did not follow his inner prompting from God. The whale swallowed him, depositing him forcefully where he had been prompted to go in the first place. The world needs each one of us to be ourselves. When we are doing something not ours to do, we are in the way of the person who needs to be expressing himself or herself in that place. And if we choose not to express our essence, everyone else loses the wonder and value of us.

For a man to achieve all that is demanded of him he must regard himself as greater than he is.
—Goethe

Using cargo cult religion.

In his book, Surely You're Joking Mr. Feynman, physicist Richard Feynman describes a group of South Seas natives after World War II. During the war they had seen airplanes land with lots of good things inside, such as clothes and food. After the war, they wanted those things to appear again. So they built runways, lit fires and made a wooden hut. A man sat in it wearing two wooden pieces on his head that looked like headphones. Then they waited for the planes. Of course, nothing ever happened. They had the form, not the essence. He calls this "cargo cult religion."

We do the same thing when we merely worship symbols and rituals and magic to get to God. We pray for miracles when we are the miracle. For the planes to land, we must build real runways, with real substance. This takes work—and the willingness to let go of who and what we think we are. Shifting is not a magic bullet; it is a process.

Thinking things are different when they're not.

Have you ever thought that what was bothering you had magically transformed into something different, a better picture, and then discovered it had not? Have you ever seen that something wasn't working but just "knew" that if you waited long enough it would change?

Tell the truth—you know these are both lies, don't you? And we know that lying, especially lying to ourselves, is a huge kink in the abundance-hose.

Sometimes we think things are different only because we are looking at them from a new angle. I had an example of this one day when I was roller-skating at the beach. I normally followed the same route each day. At one point the path had a fork in it. I would always take the left path. This path took me by the bay and then circled back around a park. One day I was lost in thought while skating.

Suddenly I realized that I had never before seen the bay that I was looking at. For a moment, my heart froze. I thought I was lost. Where had this bay come from? I had skated the area for years and I had never seen it before. I stopped skating and stood looking at the bay. Soon I recognized a familiar landmark and I suddenly knew what had happened. I had unconsciously taken the right-hand loop. I was seeing from the opposite direction.

Later that day I applied this insight to a personal relationship. I had been dating a new man whom I thought was very different from the last one. I had left the previous relationship because it had become emotionally abusive. This new man looked different, he came from a different background, and therefore I felt he treated me differently. I stopped by his office to pick him up, but for some reason I found myself extremely irritated and upset with him. I excused myself and went to the bathroom. As I looked into the mirror, I remembered the skating incident from that morning. A light bulb went on in my head and I realized that although this man seemed different, he was not.

I was in the same type of situation from which I had just freed myself. Nothing had changed at all. I had merely been imagining that the situation was new.

Pay attention to those things in your life that you think will get better, or that you think have gotten better even though you have not done any changing yourself. For things to "change" we must face the truth about what they are and what we want, and not be afraid to move on if necessary.

Express your purpose through work, job, business, career.

Your soul doesn't care what you do for a living—and when your life is over, neither will you. Your soul cares only about what you're being while you're doing what you're doing.
—Neale Donald Walsch

"Everyone does God's work in their own way," Wright told a rival, "You do it your way, I do it in His."
—Frank Lloyd Wright

The more we live by our intellect, the less we understand the meaning of Life.
—Leo Tolstoy

Trust thyself, every heart vibrates to that iron string. Accept the place the divine providence has found for you, the society of your contemporaries, the connection of events. Great men have always done so, and confided themselves childlike to the genius of their age, betraying their perception that the Eternal was stirring at their heart.
—Ralph Waldo Emerson

Although we often express ourselves through our work, we do not own our work. We don't succumb to the temptation to say, "This is my work."

No matter how wonderful that work is, when we claim it as ours it now owns us and we have forgotten to put God First. Our "work" is to express God's love and express the unique qualities that make up our individuality. Since this is who you are, you are never "out of work." This is nice to know because it makes unemployment impossible.

If we find ourselves out of human work, the need is not to heal an adverse situation. The need is to practice what we know—that our work is to express who we are. On a moment-by-moment basis we acknowledge the evidence of Love, and Love will provide the ways and means to supply us with our human needs.

Principle, One Mind, does not analyze symptoms such as being out of work. It simply perceives Its own presence and power. To us this will appear as ideas accepted and to be acted upon.

We can always experience strength, security, and stability if we will look away from the prevalent and pervasive claim that we have no value, and instead remember that there is no other power to resist Principle. All activities are the activities of the One Mind and those activities are what we call "business."

During one of my "job searches," I kept wishing that God was much more direct in sending messages to me. I wished It would just send me a fax and let me know what the heck I was do. Finally, I got that fax, and I am passing it on to you:

Dear Loved One,

You have been reassigned to a new position. It is the one I have been telling you about for many years. It meets all the criteria that you asked for. In addition, your pay scale has been elevated to meet your new understanding of your worth.

I have been holding this position open for you for quite some time, since you are the only one who can do this particular job. I felt that you were ready a few years ago, but as we discussed, you felt that you had other things to do, and what you wish is what I want for you.

Today I rejoice that you have finally agreed to accept this new position. As you are performing your tasks, please remember that the ease and enjoyment you experience are sure signs that you are doing a wonderful job.

Please call on me at any time for assistance and encouragement, or if you wish to extend your job description. You may also contact me if you desire to increase your salary, which will be my pleasure to do.

Your ever-loving employer and Father-Mother, God

Love where you are.

To affect the quality of the day, that is the highest of arts. Every man is tasked to make his life, even in its details, worthy of the contemplation of his most elevated and critical hour.
—Henry David Thoreau, Walden

Remember that marvelous TV Show Quantum Leap? The show revolved around the premise that the main character had somehow perfected time travel. The problem was he couldn't get back to his own time.

Instead, when he traveled in time he would "leap" into someone's life, become that character until his assignment was complete, and then "leap" into another time and person. Sometimes he would think that he had completed his assignment but the leap wouldn't happen. At that point he would look again to see what he had missed and continue to live that life as well as he could until the issue was truly resolved—and at that point he would leap.

Sometimes we are stuck in a place that we really don't like and nothing seems to get us out of it. The emotions of hate or dislike are like glue, and won't let us go.

As a young mother, I lived in a town that I had grown to dislike very much. I thought about how much I wanted to "get out of there," but no opportunities or money presented themselves to make the move. With each day that went by, I counted more reasons why I didn't like where I was. One day I drove the car I disliked (because it too reminded me of the place I lived), to the store. As I was pulling away from the curb, someone pulled up behind me and hit my car. I got out and looked at the person who had run into me and started to laugh. He represented everything I disliked about where I lived. I had finally gotten the message from my Angel Ideas, even though they had to be pretty graphic and hard-hitting for me to wake up.

I went home and decided to make where we lived as beautiful as possible. Since I was short on funds, I took my shovel and dug up the entire front yard by hand—and replaced it with a brick walk, fencing, and flowers. I then did the same in back. I soon loved where I was living, and when I did leap to the next place I had forgotten how much I disliked the old one.

A calling is a messenger of change.
—Greg Levoy, Callings

You miss 100% of the shots you never take.
—Wayne Gretsky

Where is your focus?

It is not enough to stay busy. So, too, are the ants. The question is: What are you busy doing?
—Henry David Thoreau

The idea of Shifting is easy. Even the doing of Shifting is easy. Why we sometimes remain in low gear is that we simply forget the basics. If you ever find yourself in a place where you need a quick visual to Shift out of low gear, try this picture.

Pretend you are at the movies. All of a sudden the movie on the screen starts to sputter and fade. Eventually you can't hear or understand anything. At that moment, does anyone in the audience jump up and run to the screen and try to fix the picture? No, the whole audience turns around and yells at the person in the projection room, "Focus the projector!"

We are all sitting in the movies watching our lives unfold. When we do not like the picture, there's no point in running to the screen (our life) and beating on it. Instead, stop and focus the projector (your thinking).

This focusing will change the picture. And if you yearn to be everything that you've dreamed of and want your life to unfold with meaning and joy, focus your projector on the image of the Infinite Loving One—and your life will overflow with peace and abundance.

Eventually you will notice that you are not the movie, the projector, or the One who does the focusing. In the meantime, Shifting to God First will start the wheels moving, and the power of perception will take you where you want to go.

PRACTICAL PURPOSE.

Here is one last worksheet for you. Write out what you want your purpose, as expressed in a life career, to feel and look like, after starting with a qualities list. Finish up with an I Choose list and then give it back to God. So Be It.

Once you have completed the qualities list put the words into a story about how you want to spend your life. Be sure to include people, places, things, activities, and feelings.

The qualities I desire to express in my career are:

1. _____
2. _____
3. _____
4. _____
5. _____
6. _____
7. _____
8. _____

This is a story of how I want to spend my life:

Chapter Seventeen: The 7th Step To Shift

The Seventh Step—Celebrate with Gratitude

At the end of each ever-expanding circle of our increasing awareness that we live in the Kingdom of Heaven, we celebrate with gratitude—for what we now know, understand, and have put into practice, of Truth.

Our gratitude is unending for the understanding that as we Shift to Spiritual Perception and focus on Truth, what is untrue is revealed and easily dissolved through the understanding that all that has ever happened or will happen is the activity of the One Mind.

We remind ourselves that the purpose of the Shift to Spiritual Perception is not to change the outside picture, but to know and experience and be the activity of God.

Use these following statements of Truth as guidelines to stay on the Spiritual path: I know that what I perceive to be reality magnifies. Therefore, I am willing to choose to magnify only GRACIOUS.

God First: I will put God First in everything that I say, think, or do.

Repent: I will change my thinking and Shift to Spiritual Perception.

Angel Ideas: I will listen for, and take action on, the constant guidance of Angel Ideas that reveal light, love, and abundance.

Choose Consciously: I choose to be conscious of the good in my life that has already been provided through the activity of the unlimited Mind of God, the only Cause and Creator.

Imagine—What If: I will imagine only the feelings of what is beautiful, good, pure, and true.

Obsessive Vigilance: I will be obsessive about only one thing: Shifting to GRACIOUS.

Unkink The Hose: I will Unkink the constantly flowing abundance-hose by releasing negative habits, limited belief systems, and personality.

So Be It: I will give it to God when I have done my part; and having done all I will stand in Love.

I acknowledge in gratitude and joy that all of my life is in the constant care of a loving, all-good God.

So Be It.

Author's Note

Writing this book was a culmination of having people ask me for advice throughout my life, based on my point of view. This point of view "came with me," but has been refined through practice and thought and by reading every book about God and spirituality and philosophy that I could lay my hands on, driven by my deep need to search for Truth.

It was the urging of friends that prompted me to solidify what I was telling them and to begin to offer a class called The Shift, and it was friends who then said, "Please write this down in a book," and that's how this book, *Living In Grace* was born. It was a long gestation period. It took over eight years to write. It was originally published in 2002. I have updated a few things each time it has been republished, but nothing that most people would notice.

If you like what I write, you can help spread the word, and keep my work going, by "liking" my books on Amazon, and anywhere else the option is offered. I would be honored if you would also post your honest reviews of the book. This will help other readers decide whether it is worth their reading time.

In today's world it is the reader that spreads the word about books they like. If you like mine, anyway you choose to spread the word will be so helpful and appreciated. I thank you in advance for all that you do!

I hope this book has helped you discover more about the Truth of yourself, and that your life will expand in wonderful ways because of this knowledge.

Join my mailing list and get another book in *The Shift Series* for free, *The Daily Shift*.

This book is packed with seven-day practice sessions for everything from money, health, or love. So many you can practice for over half a year, before repeating yourself.

Join me here: https://becalewis.com/spiritual-self-help

Plus, I run often run contests, and if you are on the list, you might be a lucky winner!

Looking forward to getting to know you!

-Beca

PS

You can find the money sheets for downloading here:

https://www.becalewis.com/books/shift-series/grace/

ACKNOWLEDGMENTS

My heartfelt thanks to everyone who has ever read this book and shared it and to *The Women's Council* at The Shift who continue to study and support the ideas found within this book. Every day I am grateful for all of you.

More Ways To Connect

Connect with me online:
http://www.facebook.com/becalewiscreative
https://www.facebook.com/groups/becalewisfans/
http://instagram.com/becalewis
http://www.linkedin.com/in/becalewis
https://www.goodreads.com/BecaLewis -
http://www.pinterest.com/theshift/
http://www.twitter.com/becalewis
http://www.facebook.com/becalewis

OTHER BOOKS BY BECA

The Shift Series - Spiritual Self-Help
Living in Grace: The Shift to Spiritual Perception
The Daily Shift: Daily Lessons From Love To Money
The 4 Essential Questions: Choosing Spiritually
Healthy Habits
The 28 Day Shift To Wealth: A Daily Prosperity Plan
The Intent Course: Say Yes To What Moves You

The Karass Chronicles - Paranormal Mystery
Karass
Pragma
Jatismar
Exousia
Stemma
Paragnosis

The Return To Erda Series - Fantasy
Shatterskin
Deadsweep
Abbadon

The Chronicles of Thamon - Fantasy
Banished
Betrayed
Discovery

Perception Parables: - Fiction - very short stories
Love's Silent Sweet Secret: A Fable About Love
Golden Chains And Silver Cords: A Fable About
Letting Go

Advice: - Nonfiction

A Woman's ABC's of Life: Lessons in Love, Life and Career from Those Who Learned The Hard WayAdvice: - Nonfiction

A Woman's ABC's of Life: Lessons in Love, Life and Career from Those Who Learned The Hard Way

ABOUT BECA LEWIS

Beca writes books that she hopes will change people's perceptions of themselves and the world, and open possibilities to things and ideas that are waiting to be seen and experienced.

At sixteen, Beca founded her own dance studio. Later, she received a Master's Degree in Dance in Choreography from UCLA and founded the Harbinger Dance Theatre, a multimedia dance company, while continuing to run her dance school.

After graduating—to better support her three children—Beca switched to the sales field, where she worked as an employee and independent contractor to many industries, excelling in each while perfecting and teaching her Shift® system, and writing books.

She joined the financial industry in 1983 and became an Associate Vice President of Investments at a major stock brokerage firm, and was a licensed Certified Financial Planner for more than twenty years.

This diversity, along with a variety of life challenges, helped fuel the desire to share what she's learned by writing and talking with the hope that it will make a difference in other people's lives.

Beca grew up in State College, PA, with the dream of becoming a dancer and then a writer. She carried that dream forward as she fulfilled a childhood wish by moving to Southern California in 1969. Beca told her family she would never move back to the cold.

After living there for thirty years, she met her

husband Delbert Lee Piper, Sr., at a retreat in Virginia, and everything changed. They decided to find a place they could call their own which sent them off traveling around the United States. For a year or so they lived and worked in a few different places before returning to live in the cold once again near Del's family in a small town in Northeast Ohio, not too far from State College.

When not working and teaching together, they love to visit and play with their combined family of eight children and five grandchildren, read, study, do yoga or taiji, feed birds, work in their garden, and design things. Actually, designing things is what Beca loves to do. Del enjoys the end result.

Made in the USA
Columbia, SC
07 November 2020

24096003R00153